W9-CMU-705

FAITH IN SEARCH OF UNDERSTANDING

JOHN B. MAGEE

GRADED PRESS
NASHVILLE, TENNESSEE

FAITH IN SEARCH OF UNDERSTANDING

A study book

Copyright © 1968 by Graded Press

All rights reserved

A publication of The Methodist Church prepared by the General Board of Education through the Editorial Division and published by. Graded Press, the curriculum publishing department of The Methodist Publishing House, 201 Eighth Ave., So., Nashville, Tennessee 37203. Printed in the United States of America.

Unless otherwise noted Scripture quotations are from the Revised Standard Version of the Bible copyright 1946 and 1952 by the Division of Christian Education of the National Council of Churches, and used by permission.

☐ Henry M. Bullock is editor of church school publications, Editorial Division, Methodist Board of Education.
☐ Horace R. Weaver is editor of adult publications.
☐ Harold L. Fair is editor of Foundation Studies in Christian Faith, the series of which *Faith in Search of Understanding* is the fourth book.

TO KATHRYN

CONTENTS

EDITOR'S INTRODUCTION

The book you are now reading is the fourth study book in a new curriculum series, Foundation Studies in Christian Faith. A new part (or unit) will be issued three months from the publication of this part and for each succeeding three months until eight parts have been published. The other seven parts are described on the inside front cover of this book. The series—Foundation Studies in Christian Faith— therefore is an eight-part study that may extend for two years if a new part is begun every three months.

The components. There are three "components" to each part of the study:

—the study book (which you are now reading)

—the book of selected readings

—the resource packet for leaders of adult groups

These three components make up one part. Each three months a new study book, a new book of selected readings, and a new resource packet for leaders of adult groups will be issued. The three components in each quarterly part have the same title. For example, the book of selected readings and the resource packet to accompany this book are also entitled *Faith in Search of Understanding.*

The study book. As you turn through this study book, you will notice several distinguishing features. At the beginning of each chapter, reference is made to several biblical passages. Read these passages in your Bible before you read the chapter. We recommend the *Oxford Annotated Bible,* Revised Standard Version (Oxford University Press) or the *Harper Study Bible,* Revised Standard Version (Zondervan Publishing House) for home use by every member of the class. (Available from Cokesbury.) Bible study is an important part of this unit. Members of the group might be asked to bring their own Bibles or the group might purchase inexpensive copies and have them available at the place of meeting for each session.

When you come to an asterisk (*) , turn to the end of the chapter. There you will find the notes which give the source of the quotations.

Leadership procedures. You will notice as you look through this book that certain paragraphs have a small black square (■) at the beginning. These paragraphs suggest a wide variety of ways of reacting to the ideas raised in the material. It is not expected that a group will use every suggestion or procedure. The procedures are placed in the study book to encourage each member of the group to assume responsibility for discussion and to stimulate thinking as you read the book. There is no separate book for leaders only. Leaders and other members of the group should each have personal copies of both the study book and the book of selected readings. Only the designated leader or "teaching team," however, will receive the resource packet described below for use with the group. The packet contains a leaders' guide.

On the first page of each chapter, reference is made to an "assignment chart." This chart may be on a sheet of poster-

8

board or newsprint or a chalkboard. It might suggest, for instance, a question to think about before the session begins. At the first session, the leader might explain to the group that he will have the chart prepared and posted before each session so that preparation for the discussion can begin as soon as each member arrives.

At the end of each chapter the suggestion is made that the leader be ready to make assignments for the next session and that members of the group be prepared to accept such assignments. Advance assignments increase the ability of the group to make the most efficient use possible of the discussion period. These assignments also suggest a variety of ways to get before the group information not included in the text itself, such as the opinions of persons outside the group or relevant facts regarding your local community or church. To make the most profitable use of assignments, the leader or leadership team should go through the entire book in their planning in order to work out which assignments would be most valuable for the group.

Leaders are not expected to use *every* procedure in this book. A large number of procedures are suggested in order that the leader and the group may *choose* those most interesting and revelant to them. A word of caution: every procedure in the book assumes that the members of the group are familiar with the text. If members have not read the text, many procedures will lose most of their significance and meaning. Encourage every member of the group to read the assigned portion of this book (and the relevant sections of the book of selected readings if the group is using that book) *in advance* of the session. Valuable discussion time is lost if the text has not been read in advance.

When small group discussion is suggested, the leader should ask each small group to choose a leader before the discussion begins. This person will be responsible for keeping the discussion "on the track" and assigning someone to

9

report to the whole group if such reporting is expected. Small groups with a responsible designated leader will be more likely to fulfill their assignment than a leaderless group.

The leader or leadership team should also note as they prepare before the beginning of the study which supplies will be needed. Someone should be designated to have the supplies at the place of meeting at the proper time. These supplies might include a chalkboard, chalk, and an eraser; or a newsprint pad and dark crayon or other type of marker; Bibles; and other materials at the discretion of the leader. (A newsprint pad, an inexpensive pad of rough paper available from most stationery stores, has the advantage of being portable.)

The book of selected readings. Each person in the group should have a copy of the book of selected readings with the same title as this study book, *Faith in Search of Understanding.* In the book of selected readings, you will find a wide variety of selections from a number of other printed resources relevant to the study of Christian theology as witness to the good news. While it is not absolutely essential for every person to have a copy of the book of selected readings, the study will be significantly enriched if this study book and the book of selected readings are read and used together. They are companion volumes. Many procedures involve use of selected readings. In this study book you will frequently see the abbreviation *S/R* followed by a number. When you come to a place in the text where this abbreviation appears, turn to the book of selected readings and find the reading whose number corresponds to the one following the abbreviation *S/R.* The book of selected readings has no page numbers —rather, the selections are numbered. Reading and discussion of these selections will greatly increase understanding of this unit.

The resource packet. In addition to a new study book and a new book of selected readings each three months, a resource packet for leaders will be issued, having the same title as the study book and the book of selected readings. Each group will need one packet with the same title as this study book, *Faith in Search of Understanding*. Each packet contains a variety of resources for use by the leader with the group: filmslips, records, pictures, maps, charts, and the like. The packet also contains a leaders' guide to suggest how the materials in the packet may best be used with the group. Each person in the group should have a study book and a book of selected readings; but only one packet will be needed for the group.

The editorial team that developed this unit was Mary Alice Asbury (manuscript editor), Harold D. Minor (leadership procedures), Nellie Moser (leadership procedures and resource packet), Lon A. Speer (resource packet), Horace R. Weaver, and Judith Weidman (book of selected readings). Dan Brawner and Richard Elliott were responsible for the design and layout. Mrs. Jeanne Arnold faithfully typed and retyped the manuscript.

HAROLD L. FAIR

AUTHOR'S PREFACE

This book represents a commitment to the value of reason for the life of faith. I do not believe that faith needs reason in order to establish or prove itself. As we shall see, it is really the other way around—faith is the ground for thought. But we need the clear light of thought in order to understand what our faith really means. Hence the title: *Faith in Search of Understanding.*

My desire is to examine the meaning of the Christian faith—not some caricature of it. In doing this I want to take my stand alongside any Christian—of whatever shade of belief—who has been loyal to that faith in the past or who is faithful to it now. We may not agree, but our faith is deeper than our reasons.

On the other hand, no man can view so grand a truth as we must study from the point of view of eternity. We all live in time and circumstance and take our perspective from some limited standpoint. What I am saying is that I realize my understanding of the Christian faith has been conditioned inescapably by certain life facts. The reader has a right to know these facts if he uses this book as a means to his own understanding. I am an ordained Methodist minister, following a tradition as son and grandson of Methodist ministers. After early years in the pastorate, I now follow my ministry as a university professor of philosophy and religion. These facts, plus the fact that I am a white, twentieth-century American, cannot fail to explain some bias in my views and account for blind spots in this work.

But I sincerely desire to move as freely beyond the limitations of my own background as is humanly possible. I want to give as reasonable and universal an accounting of the Christian faith as lies within my powers. With this in my mind I have opened myself to the amazing variety of Christian thought, past and present.

Also, because I believe that all things are ours in Christ, I have for many years studied with growing sympathy evidences of the divine Presence in the non-Christian faiths. Following the New Testament admonition to bring every thought captive to Christ, I have tried to understand modern man's quest for the meaning of existence in the arts, sciences, literature, and philosophy. A modern understanding of the Christian faith will depend, after all, upon sharing deeply in the human enterprise and sensing the deepest longings in the hearts of men. The gospel, I believe, is a response to those longings by the divine Love that is alone adequate to them.

You are invited to journey with me on this quest for understanding. I pray that our traveling together will be profitable not only to us, but to a world sorely in need of this faith.

JOHN B. MAGEE

University of Puget Sound
Tacoma, Washington

DEPARTMENT OF HOUSING AND URBAN DEVELOPMENT

Anything that keeps us from growing into the kind of persons God intended is sin.

Read these selections in your Bible:
John 1:17
Truth (as well as grace) comes through Jesus Christ.

John 18:37-38
Pilate asks, "What is truth?"

John 14:6, 16-17
Jesus *is* the truth. The Spirit *is* the truth.

1

□□

DOING THEOLOGY

"How do we reach this truth? 'By doing it,' is the answer of the Fourth Gospel. This does not mean being obedient to the commandments, accepting them and fulfilling them. Doing the truth means living out of the reality which is *He* who is the truth, making His being the being of ourselves and of our world." *

"Read the Bible. It teaches you how to act. Read the hymn-book. It contains the finest poetry ever written. Read the almanac. It shows you how to figure out what the weather will be. There isn't another book that is necessary for anyone to read, and therefore I am opposed to all libraries." *

*   *   *

■ *In the room where your group is meeting, display a large poster on which are written assignments for specific preparation to be made by the members of the group before the session begins.*

Theology is a popular topic today. Pick up almost any popular magazine like the *Reader's Digest* or any newspaper and you will find some discussion of religion. Bishop Robinson's recent paperback *Honest to God* is reported to have sold more copies than any book except the Bible.

■ One procedure for each chapter suggests that your group set goals. To help you get started, the study committee or leadership team might pose a question that, on the basis of its study and planning, expresses the main concern of the chapter. Now, as a group, ask yourselves: (1) What should we learn to help us answer this question? and (2) What should we do after we have found the answer? By your answers to these two questions, you will have set your goals for learning both content and behavior. Go through these steps as you begin the study of each new chapter, using a guiding question appropriate to the chapter. A time limit should be established for the goal-setting process.

THE NEED FOR FRESH EXPLORATIONS

How can theology be meaningful in a highly complex age? Science and technology, rapid mass communication of ideas and events, the growth of mighty nations studded with huge cities, the complex relationships of nations—all these have made the understanding of life (which is the work of theology) difficult. (Selected Reading [abbreviated hereafter *S/R*], 1.)

The problem is this: How can I be a person of faith? In its social dimension the problem is: How can I be a creative and responsible participant in this strange world? How can I learn to live and relate as a human being among beings? How can we tie the concept of God's loving care to the job of keeping house, running a business, teaching school, or carpentering?

For the church the problem can be stated in this way: How can the church—the community of faith—generate a fellowship that interprets life to its members in a challenging and significant way? Or: How can such a community of faith

16

be an effective witness of God's gospel to a puzzled world? (*S/R, 2.*)

This is not the old problem of "proving the existence of God" which was found so often in the religious literature of the recent past. It is the problem of making faith *effective*, of making it capable of demonstrating its own self-verifying power in our lives. Proving the existence of God was a task for people who were very certain of many things, but uncertain of God. Our age is uncertain of almost everything. We cannot use these uncertainties to prove God. We need the gospel to enable us to live again. We need God to give life back to us, to free us somehow to work and live in the world in a triumphant way. We do not want an argument; we need a demonstration of power—or at least a sign pointing to the place where the power is. In old-fashioned language, we are lost, and we need salvation, a way out.

One main task of theology is to point the way to the release of God's power in life. This is the way to show the reality of God. It is a far harder task than the old way of doing things. We can approach it only by beginning, in at least some small way, to show the liberating power of God in personal and family life, in political and social existence, and in the affairs of the family of nations.

The world will believe us—that is, think we have made sense—only if they see that demonstration, a demonstration guided by a clearer way of thinking about the gospel. This book is an attempt to do that. I admit that it is a rash proposal. But the whole gospel promise is rash. It promises us victory in the midst of the most perplexing problems of life. God is still ruling, and he is Love, as our Lord taught and demonstrated by his life.

■ Discuss: What do you understand as the meaning of *the power of God*? What are some characteristics of God's activity? For example, you may believe that God's activity always creates unity rather than disunity. If you believe that God is in every event but perhaps limited by the situation, how can God's activity be distinguished from sheer economic power or manipulation of persons by "religious" people? How can you guard against simply tagging the social programs you happen to like as God's activity?

On the basis of your definitions of the characteristics of God's activity, discuss in pairs or groups of four persons: What signs do you see that God's power is being released in the world? Where is the power of God being demonstrated? How do you see God at work—in automation? in the political process? in the economic process? in medical advance? in your personal and family life? in international affairs? in your community?

What do I mean by reinterpreting the gospel in this way? I mean that we must see the old concepts in new ways and with new applications. Let us use an example, the old notion of *sin*. We have thought of sin as a collection of personal sins, violations of the rules of living which we were taught—do not lie, do not steal, and so on.

But we need to see that the sin troubling our world is bigger than that. Personal sin is not so much what we have done as what we have left *undone*. It is not the person we are so much as the failure to become the person we might be. We literally *are* sin. I mean that this present self is not the one intended by God. That is the reason we feel personally frustrated and anxious.

On the social side, sin means the whole organization of life that prevents men from growing into the kind of persons God intended. The existence of the Negro ghettos in our cities, for instance, is sin. Our indifference to causes of poverty and disease is sin. Our contempt and distaste for all who are not like us is sin. The organization of our social and economic life, especially in our cities, that turns men into mere working robots is sin. The tradition of international relationships that holds a growing threat of nuclear war over the heads of all mankind is sin.

Salvation means victory over sin. It means the release of power into a new person who no longer lives by his fear, greed, and guilt, but who lives by his faith. It means the discovery of the motive power and the wisdom to make headway against racial injustices, against inhuman industrial arrangements, against the tide of affairs that leads ever nearer to destruction. (S/R, 3.)

The major doubts of our age, I think, are not primarily logical. They are practical. They are doubts about whether Christianity can really do what it has talked so long about. Is there a power in human life that can lift men above the selfishness of race, class, and nation? Does faith really make any difference, or is it merely a clever disguise for failure—a smoke-screen used to conceal our despair while we hang on to the old ways which are failing?

Sin and salvation are just two examples of concepts that must be reinterpreted if the gospel is to make sense even to its own adherents. Some other concepts are revelation, atonement, incarnation, faith, and even God. I believe that each of these speaks to some basic need of human beings—to our needs. They must be liberated to speak in this way. This book attempts that task.

■ Have one person read aloud the discussion of sin and salvation in the preceding paragraphs. Then discuss in the total group: Do you agree with these ways of defining sin and salvation? Why? At what points do you disagree? Why? How do these interpretations differ from what you have been taught? What criteria do you think the author used to come to his conclusions? What criteria would you use to help you interpret the concepts of sin and salvation?

Now, in groups of four or five persons read silently S/R, 3. Then let each group define sin and salvation in light of one of the four sections of S/R, 3.

Group A will deal with the section on *Realism;* Group B, the section on *Inconsistency;* Group C, the section on *Radicalism;* and Group D, the section on *Intercession.*

Discuss in the groups: How is this description of Christian witness like what you observe of other Christians or carry out yourself? Unlike? One person from each group may share a very brief report with the entire group.

WHAT THIS BOOK IS ABOUT

This book will show how men of the past have found the freedom of life in their faith. It will show, all too briefly, how they hammered out their understanding of the events of their day in terms of the gospel and were set free to obey God in their time.

I will try to show how these same problems are being wrestled with today—because they are recurring human problems. And, hopefully, I will show how every person who reads this book can participate in this same wrestling of faith and discover the power of the gospel.

After much consultation this book was titled *Faith in Search of Understanding*. Let me explain why. A generation ago it was thought that by reason we could establish faith. Now we know better. First, principles can never be established by argument. We begin with faith. (*S/R,* 4.) The function of thought is not to establish faith but to clarify it, to bring it to a clearer understanding of itself. The faith is something given to us in the history of the church. What is meant by that?

Simply this. Something happened. Abraham heard the call of God and left his ancestral home in the Tigris and Euphrates valley and traveled on the strength of that call into Palestine. Moses heard the call of God and went down into Egypt and led the Israelite slaves into a country of their own. On the way he brought them to a mountain where a covenant between God and the people was agreed upon— God would be their God and they would be his people.

Jesus was born. He lived, suffered, died, and appeared again to his disciples. This happened. But something more also happened. The people who were associated with him in these events were changed. They found that whereas they were failing as human beings before, now they found themselves succeeding because of the new surge of life that had come to them through Jesus. Most often these were ordinary men: doubters like Thomas, rich and selfish men like Zacchaeus or Matthew, inconstant men like Peter, or emotionally violent men like James and John ("sons of thunder"). These personal changes were facts.

The church was born—a new fellowship of faith. This fellowship grew until it came from being a small sect of Jews in an unimportant country to being the faith of an empire.

We inherit this faith. It has come to us. (You will recall that the study previous to this was on the church, *We Have This Heritage.*) We can, of course, reject that faith and heritage. But it is ours for the asking. (*S/R,* 5.)

The faith is given, yes, but its *interpretation* is not given. Each age, from the very beginning, has had to wrestle with what this faith means. In the process it has moved from culture to culture, from language to language, and from race to race. Each time the meaning has had to be deciphered in terms that made sense to the new culture, in its own language, and in terms of its special problems. To be sure, the faith remains the same—but the life situations change in which this faith influences men.

Even the New Testament age did not have one single agreed upon interpretation. All interpretations pointed, to be sure, to the same Lord. They all experienced the same wonderful changes that took place in men and in their relationships to one another. Yet even within that short time the language changed from Aramaic to Greek. Before the New Testament was complete, Jerusalem the old center had been destroyed. The new faith was set adrift in the world. Such new facts had to be related intelligibly to the continuing fact of faith. Christian theology, with all its rich varieties, was born.

Faith seeking understanding is a key to the whole history of theology. (*S/R,* 6.) The faith went from the Hebrew to the Greek world. Then it moved into and conquered the Latin world. Each time it took on fresh interpretations. It began as a small sect; it became the church of an empire. New interpretations were called for. In time it moved north and converted the whole of Europe. Barbarian tribes were now Christian. They needed to understand the faith. Much later the faith spread throughout the world, coming to our own continent. Again, the faith had to seek understanding of itself in this new setting.

THEOLOGY IS THE WORK OF THE WHOLE CHURCH

You are a theologian whether you want to be or not. Every man is. This may appear to be overdoing a good thing. But every man is a scientist and philosopher, too. These scholarly forms of intellectual activity are simply refinements of common sense activities that belong to our common humanity. Theology has to do with those ultimate beliefs by which we order our lives. Every person has such beliefs, even though everyone does not spend much time thinking about them consciously. Such ultimate beliefs underlie our morality, our politics, our conduct of family and business affairs. (S/R, 7.)

The reason for appealing to each person to be a conscious theologian is simply that it is better than being an unconscious one. Bringing these basic concepts into the light for examination and critical appraisal is a way of becoming more human.

Often these basic assumptions about life are contradictory. If they are, life is caught in severe tensions and contradictions. (S/R, 8.) More often, our conduct is not consistent with our fundamental beliefs. Conscious theologizing helps to bring this inconsistency to a level of awareness. Perhaps this is one of the reasons that we resist doing theology—we resist the changes that such thinking might require in our policy of life. This much is certain, however, we cannot avoid being either good or bad theologians.

These remarks underscore the hope of this study series—
that each person will become more personally involved in
thinking about his faith and thereby strengthening and ex-
tending it.

■ Read silently, or let one person read aloud as the other members
of the group follow the reading, S/R, 8.
Discuss this question: As a person of faith, how do you feel about
the tensions and contradictions evident in the reading?
If you could talk to Harry about this situation, what might you
say to him? Let two persons role play (a spontaneous acting out of
a situation to gain insight, to learn how others feel, or to solve a
problem) the dialogue that might occur.

WHAT IS THEOLOGY?

Theology is faith seeking an understanding of itself. So-
called "systematic theology" is, as the name suggests, a treatment of the great themes of faith in such a way that they form
a coherent system of thought. This was more easily done in
the past when there were fewer questions urging themselves
on the faithful.

A more topical kind of theology seems more appropriate to
our day. This way of theologizing begins with questions that
puzzle us and then searches our faith to see what answers
it can give to our perplexity. These questions arise out of life
itself, out of our guilts and fears, out of our perplexities in
the face of social movements or schools of thought that
threaten our values and our faith. An instance of the latter
would be the presence today of so-called "youth culture" with
its questioning of conventional moral standards, its strange
forms of dress and hairdo, and its weird music and dancing.
(S/R, 9.)

Another example would be the puzzles that arise over our
(America's) relationship to communism or to the problems
that arise in the relationships of the great world powers. The
vitality of present-day theology is largely due to the fact that
it has something fundamental to say on these topics which

cannot be said from any other perspective but that of faith.

Theology is thus a form of witnessing to the good news of the gospel. How does it witness? By spelling out in terms of our immediate problems the deliverance from evil that our Lord announced—the coming of the Kingdom here and now, as well as in the future.

This is another way of saying that theology is an *existential* (see definition below) subject rather than a theoretical one. Theoretical studies, like the philosophical analysis of concepts such as "cause" or "freedom," or problems in theoretical physics concerned with the number of fundamental particles in matter, are chiefly concerned with *knowing*, that is, satisfying our curiosity. *Existential* studies are focused on the problems that arise in *existing*, in the problems we face in humanizing our own existence either socially or personally. It is not curiosity that chiefly impels us to ask existential questions, such as what sin or salvation mean. It is rather the fact that we are troubled by sin and we long for release from it. Such topics cannot be considered in a theoretical and detached way.

There are no fixed ways in which this kind of theologizing may be done. We may do it systematically as Paul Tillich has done in his three volumes of theology, or we may do it as Reinhold Niebuhr has done by discussing difficult questions in personal and international relations in biblical categories like original sin or pride. Other thinkers have done it by theologizing about liturgy or art, about prayer or social action.

The essential thing in all these efforts is what Paul Tillich calls the "correlation" between faith and life. The correlation takes place in this way. Life presents us with certain facts that perplex us. Our faith promises victory over perplexities. We then search the faith to see in what way it illuminates—"answers"—the perplexity. Naturally,

24

in this process the problems themselves are restated because they appear in a new light. Often this is the most important part of the answer we get from theology.

■ One person may be prepared to state briefly the major ideas in this section. Or take time for all persons to quickly scan the material.

Now let four or five persons phrase questions that they feel are most crucial to human existence—questions about guilts and fears, threats to values, concern over international affairs. Have someone list the questions on newsprint or chalkboard.

Let the entire group or small groups restate each question so that the word *God* appears in it. For example, a question of human existence might be: What is the meaning of life? A restatement of the problem in the light of faith might be: What does God want me to do with my life?

What implications does each question have after its restatement that it did not have before?

THE PERSPECTIVE OF THE AUTHOR

A reader has a right to know the basic point of view of an author who writes on such themes as we will discuss throughout this book.

As I said in the Preface, my essential desire is to express truly the Christian faith. I do not want to separate myself from any Christians who have been loyal to that faith throughout the ages or at the present time. My understanding of what that faith is has been conditioned by the fact that I was born into and reared in a Methodist minister's family. In due time I trained for and entered the Methodist ministry in which I now serve as a university teacher. These facts plus the fact that I am a white, twentieth-century American cannot but explain some of my views and account for some blind spots in this book.

But I do not wish to be bound by these traditions. I want to give as reasonable and as universal account of the Christian faith as lies within my powers. To help me in this enterprise I have therefore exposed myself to the wide range of Christian thought in the history of our faith as well as having sympathetically studied the non-Christian religions.

I have tried, moreover, to understand modern man and his quest for some kind of authentic existence as this search reveals itself in the arts, sciences, and humanities. This, I believe, is necessary because our understanding of the faith will depend upon sharing deeply in the human enterprise and feeling the deep longings of the hearts of men. The gospel is fundamentally a response to those longings by the Love that alone is adequate to them.

You are then invited to journey with me into this quest for the understanding of our faith. We will begin in the next section with the way in which this quest shows itself in the history of our Christian past, beginning with the first Christian community.

■ Let persons in the group attempt to express or clarify their understanding of faith by completing the following sentences. The leadership team should have paper and pencils available.

Faith is ⸺⸺⸺⸺⸺⸺⸺⸺⸺⸺

Faith is like ⸺⸺⸺⸺⸺⸺⸺⸺⸺

Faith enables me to ⸺⸺⸺⸺⸺⸺⸺

Faith may be seen ⸺⸺⸺⸺⸺⸺⸺⸺

Faith keeps me from ⸺⸺⸺⸺⸺⸺⸺

Faith requires of me ⸺⸺⸺⸺⸺⸺⸺

If time allows, some persons may wish to share what they have written. It would be interesting for individuals to keep what they have written and, then, after studying this unit, complete the same sentences. Compare the two statements to see what, if any, changes have come about in their understanding and expression of the meaning of faith.

■ To gain experience in "doing theology," individual members of the class might wish to keep a theological diary during the study. A medium-sized loose leaf notebook would be convenient. At the end of each day think over the events of the day. Choose one event and attempt to write down a theological interpretation of it. That is, put into your own words your understanding of the event in terms of the gospel.

■ As a benediction, pray together "God Be in My Head" (Resource Packet, item 1).

> God be in my head,
>   And in my understanding;
> God be in mine eyes
>   And in my looking;
> God be in my mouth,
>   And in my speaking;
> God be in my heart,
>   And in my thinking;
> God be at mine end,
>   And at my departing. Amen.

■ Let the leadership team be prepared to give assignments for the next chapter of study and the members of the group be prepared to accept the assignments.

NOTES ON CHAPTER 1

Page 15: Paul Tillich, *The New Being* (Charles Scribner's Sons, 1955), page 71. Copyright 1955 by Paul Tillich. Used by permission.

Page 15: From a speech of a Georgia Assemblyman, quoted in Richard P. Hofstadter, *Anti-Intellectualism in American Life* (Alfred A. Knopf, 1963), page 125. Copyright © 1962, 1963 by Richard P. Hofstadter. Used by permission.

PAUL DUCKWORTH

Has modern civilization made dependence upon God no longer necessary?

Read these selections in your Bible:
1 Corinthians 12:4-6, 12-14
God inspires a variety of services.

Ephesians 6:13-17
Paul advises the *whole* armor of God.

Colossians 1:15-20
Christ is the clue to the invisible God.

1 Corinthians 3:1-11, 18-23
Do not be misled by controversies.
All truth is yours in Christ.

2

□□

VARIETIES OF
NEW TESTAMENT THEOLOGY

"Now, this is the greatest evil that the division of the church has brought forth; it raises in every communion a selfish, partial orthodoxy, which consists in courageously defending all that it has, and condemning all that it has not. . . . And yet I will venture to say that if each church could produce but one man apiece that had the piety of an apostle and the impartial love of the first Christians in the first church at Jerusalem, that a Protestant and a Papist [Roman Catholic] of this stamp would not want half a sheet of paper to hold their articles of union, nor be half an hour before they were of one religion." *

*   *   *

■ *As you arrive at your place of meeting, check the assignment chart for specific preparation to be made before the session begins.*
■ *Set goals for your study of this chapter as suggested on page 16.*

I truly believe that the unity of the New Testament can be expressed in Paul's phrase that "God was in Christ reconciling the world to himself." But differences emerge the moment we ask, How was God in Christ? Or how did God's presence in Christ reconcile the world? Or how does it affect the lives of men? Here are we in the realm of theological interpretation.

The biblical writers suggest the presence of God in Christ in various ways. Jesus was the Messiah, says Mark. Jesus was the pre-existent Son of God who came down from heaven, writes Paul in Colossians. Jesus was the divine word who became flesh, says the Gospel of John. Jesus was the new High Priest by direct ordination of God, writes the author of the Letter to the Hebrews.

Here is the unity in variety that I am trying to make clear. They all agree that God was in Christ in a very special way, meeting the deepest needs of man. But they turn to images and concepts of many different sorts in order to interpret that fact in all its mysterious richness. (*S/R*, 10.)

Another way of putting this same point is to say that the original faith combined two features—a proclamation and a teaching (a way of life). The *proclamation* announced the good news of a divinely ordained person whom God had raised from the dead and given a unique place in his dealings with humanity. The teaching—given, as Matthew says, from the Mount, just as Moses had brought the Ten Commandments from Sinai—was an ethical way of life for all men who pressed into God's divine kingdom.

The whole of the New Testament is a commentary on this proclamation and this teaching. It is a book that gives wide room for interpretation within the community which holds loyally to the faith once delivered to the apostles.

■ The unity of the gospel message of the New Testament is expressed in Colossians 1:15-20. You might begin this session by having

30

one person read this Scripture. Then listen as another reads 1 Corinthians 3:1-11. What insights from the Corinthian passage can help you in understanding the message of Colossians 1:15-20?

WHY THIS VARIETY?

Would it not have been better if there had been only the unity and not the variety? Would not that have prevented all this separation into sects and churches? We might think so at times. A living faith, however, never can have that kind of unity. (S/R, 11.)

Take the political faith that Americans have in democracy. Think of the varieties of interpretation that this concept has had in the history of our country. Would it even now be possible to get a majority of Americans to agree on some single statement as to what democracy really is? Not likely. As long as democracy is a living social faith, it will continue to express itself in a wide variety of political and social beliefs covering a wide spectrum of convictions from very conservative to very liberal.

No wonder then that the faith created by Jesus Christ should have expressed itself in many ways. The original events of the faith occurred in Palestine under the special circumstances of the Hebrew people as wards of the Roman government. But its vitality soon sent it deep into Europe and Africa. In these new circumstances, as well as in its Palestinian homeland, it took root and grew.

Explanations that were suitable for one place were not adequate for another. If it was to become a world faith, it had to put down its roots in a variety of places, cultures, and races. It is this fact which required new theologies, new interpretations in the language and understanding of the new people who were hearing the gospel preached. In one word, the advantage of these new interpretations was *relevance*.

But the desire for relevance has a danger. Translating the faith into terms understandable to a given people and time may subtly alter the substance of the faith and distort the gospel. Every new interpretation has to be continually tested against the primitive faith to make sure that essential elements have not been omitted or changed beyond recognition. This is why the New Testament is important to us—it expresses the original faith along with a great variety of permissible interpretations. It is a guide both to the unity and variety of our thought.

The best way to minimize this danger is to recognize it as a natural hazard which Christians in every age must run. With each new interpretation we must ask: Is this the gospel of Jesus Christ, or is it some other gospel of merely human invention?

The greatness of the New Testament is that in its *unity* it speaks of the faith itself, and in its *variety* it invites men to ceaselessly make that faith relevant to new situations as they arise. It is a book of freedom and variety inviting each new group to enter a dialogue bent on giving an even more significant interpretation of the faith itself. (*S/R*, 12.)

■ Use *S/R*, 10, 11, and 12 to guide the class in reflecting upon the preceding paragraphs. Study the readings one at a time. Each person will need a pencil. As one person reads aloud, others will follow the reading marking ideas that provide new insights into the ways the New Testament writers understood Jesus, statements that raise questions in their minds about how the unity of the gospel message can be maintained while interpretations constantly change, and clues to how the Bible invites reinterpretation. Have a period of open discussion. To allow as many persons as possible to participate, each person should speak only once until all have had opportunity to speak.

WE UNDERSTAND OURSELVES THROUGH HISTORY

One of the things which the Bible makes most clear to us is that our faith is historical in nature. We cannot understand it except through history, that is, how God has revealed himself in the lives of men and the events of nations. Buddhism or Hinduism can ignore history, because it is not important to these faiths. But Christians believe that God created the world with a purpose and that God has shown that purpose in history. The Bible is a unique sample of history in which that purpose is made most plain. Here the Eternal's purpose lies open to view. (S/R, 13.)

But God's purpose is not limited to Hebrew history; it extends to all peoples everywhere. The key is in the Bible, yes, but it unlocks doors for modern Americans and Russians too. Or at least so we Christians believe. We cannot make this point very well, however, unless we are willing to study the purposes of God in history to sharpen our insight and test our faith.

All this may sound as though it is mainly a study for statesmen or leaders of nations. After all, what can the average man do about these large-scale purposes that pervade historical events? This remark fails to take into account the way in which everyman's own intimate self-understanding depends upon his view of history.

Take, for instance, modern Americans like ourselves. Part of the meaning of our lives is the meaning of twentieth-century democracy in America. We cannot hope to find the full meaning of our lives apart from the significance of the events that are happening in and through our nation. Every day we answer questions about what we should do by referring to the dimension of what could be called the "meaning of being an American." And we feel personal shame or pride in the actions of our country. (S/R, 14.) march at Selma

But being an American is not enough. There are other nations too; we are a very small, even though influential, minority in the world. We are more than Americans; we are human beings. The meaning of history at which the Bible aims is the meaning of man's history as man. It is not limited to being a Jew or a Roman or an Englishman or an American.

33

The reason why the faith of the Bible is suited to men of every culture is that the meaning of *being human* is more important than the significance of any group or nation. (*S/R*, 15.)

■ Study the cartoon (*S/R*, 15) . What is the main character's view of himself? Assuming that one's self-understanding depends on one's view of history, what would you say is this man's view of history? On the basis of his interpretation of his situation, what is his understanding of the meaning of *being human?* What is his basis for his final conclusion? If you were in his place, how would your views differ from his as you see them?

FINDING GOD IN CONCRETE EVENTS

But why all this study? This is a natural question. If the faith is such a grand meaning, why bother to study it? Why not just announce it, publish it abroad? The reason is that the meaning of history is embedded in the events of the past; and only prayerful interpretation can bring that meaning out into the clear. This process of interpretation of the past is the primary work of theology.

Since God's primary revelation is in concrete events, we must learn to translate into modern terms, for instance, what God was doing in and through Moses. One answer is that he is liberating people as he liberated the children of Israel from Egypt. But what are the forms of slavery in our day? Unemployment? Segregation? Hunger? Ignorance? Prejudice? To which Egypt is he sending us that we might, like Moses, help to bring more freedom to man?

Only a careful reading of the Bible story, thoughtfully and prayerfully interpreted, can answer that question. Centuries after Moses, the prophet Amos reminded the Israelites that God had been delivering her enemies from their captivities as well. Yet Moses was not sent to deliver the Moabites or the Syrians; he was sent to the Israelites—to one situation only.

My point is simply this. We must reconsider the great events in which God was clearly involved in the Bible—such as the coming of Jesus Christ—and try to find out what he is saying to *us* through these events. Great insights emerge, such as this: God is the great liberator. But what that means concretely for us can only come through our becoming, like Moses, a student of the will of God in our own concrete situation. (*S/R,* 16.) The will of God is not *an* answer to a particular question, but a frame of reference in which to seek an answer. When we find that, we will discover that we belong to the fellowship of the faithful in which such men as Moses and Amos appear.

■ Look at the forms of slavery listed on page 34. What other forms of slavery would you add to the list? Let one person write your suggestions on chalkboard or newsprint as they are given.

Now form groups of four to six persons. Let each group select one of the forms of slavery listed. Talk for a few minutes about your understanding of God's will for individuals. Does God intend for all persons to develop as distinct persons? In what ways? What is your understanding of equality of all persons? What freedoms are necessary for the maximum development of the individual?

Work together to develop a paragraph stating what your group considers to be God's will concerning the form of slavery you are dealing with. How does your statement compare with the statement of the mission of Christ as seen in Luke 4:18-19?

Have one person from your group read your paragraph for the entire group. On the basis of the paragraphs, discuss the question: What does God require of me/us in relation to these problems?

■ Slavery comes in many forms. Study the pictures in Bulletin Board Display II (Resource Packet, item 2). How would you answer the question that accompanies the pictures? See the Leaders' Guide in the packet for directions for assembling the display and for suggestions to guide your discussion.

■ How can we understand the will of God? Read silently *S/R,* 16. Discuss in the total group: The will of God is not a particular answer but rather a frame of reference in which to seek answers. How do you respond to this idea? Does it surprise you? shock you? free you? Does it help you in your understanding of the will of God? How? Is the will of God to be sought in every situation? Why? Why not? Can every decision be traced back to an underlying value? Give evidence to support your answer. How can we use the idea of the "will of God" to help us make decisions about events? For example, if God wills justice for all, how should our decisions be made?

FINDING GOD IN EVENTS TODAY

Has modern civilization made dependence upon God no longer necessary? On the one hand, think of the tremendous development of education, industrial production, and the expanding means of life granted to us by modern science. Should we set ancient faiths aside and go ahead on our own? We do indeed seem to possess the means for transforming the world.

Yet think, on the other hand, for a moment of how we are using these means—to pollute the air and water, to change cities into growing slums, and even threaten to cremate all of life with our atomic arsenals.

Even in comfort and affluence, millions of people are desperately unhappy and feel that life has failed them. Civilization does not save men; it only seems to provide more ways of being lost. You cannot find a path out of a deep forest by increasing the number of trees or even the number of paths. We need a sign pointing, "Here lies thy path." This is what I mean when I speak of a "meaning" for life. Faith could be such a sign—if we could only decipher it.

But even if this is true, Christianity may seem to be irrelevant to modern life. What I mean is that technology has produced huge cities, enormous populations, great political powers, and unlimited industrial development. These things are new to our planet. In these difficulties God may seem irrelevant—especially a God from the ancient past. How can a faith that began in a world so different from ours have anything to say to the complex problems we face? (*S/R*, 17.)

■ *S/R*, 17 is a proposal by a group of persons (not sponsored by a church) of ways to meet the needs of people in our cities. Every attempt to be relevant to the needs of people is influenced by the conscious or unconscious value assumptions or opinions of the persons attempting to meet the needs.

Working in groups of four or five persons, study the reading carefully. Analyze each section ·by asking: On what value assumptions about persons are these proposals made? How can you relate these values to the will of God? Are the proposals compatible with, derived from, or in opposition to, the will of God?

Caution: This discussion should not become involved with expressions of agreement or disagreement with the proposals. Your concern is simply to try to discover the view of the value of the individual held by the persons who made the proposals.

If we are to make the faith effective today, we must do the work of theology. What is the work of theology? To find a fresh interpretation of the faith for modern circumstances. This can be partly accomplished by going over the past to see how such new interpretations can be made without changing the substance of the original faith itself.

From the theologians of the New Testament, the early Roman and Greek thinkers, the great figures of the Reformation, and those who tried to adapt the faith to what has happened since the rise of modern science, we can learn how to make the faith relevant to our day. *(S/R, 18.)*

■ New Testament writers used various images to interpret the gospel to their readers.

Interested persons in your group might work as a team during the coming week to find some modern images that would reinterpret the faith in terms of today's world.

The team may proceed in this manner: (1) Look through the New Testament to find words that symbolize an aspect of the gospel as taught by Jesus. For example, the Door. (2) Search magazines, newspapers, and periodicals for pictures that may be used to reinterpret some aspect of the gospel message. Or members of the team may wish to draw or paint or sculpt their own interpretations. (3) The pictures could be arranged under a suitable heading on a bulletin board. Or team members might back the pictures with cardboard, cut to desired shape, and use to construct a mobile to hang in the classroom. (See *Adult Teacher,* June, July, August, 1968, for help in constructing a mobile.)

Allow time in the following session for interpretation of and reaction to the pictures chosen.

HOW THE NEW TESTAMENT EXPRESSES UNITY THROUGH VARIETY

Christendom has shown a great variety of theological opinion. But it has not been very successful—especially in the last three centuries—in coming to any substantial unity. Fortunately, the movement toward unity that is sweeping the major divisions of Christendom is partially changing the picture. Nonetheless, many denominations still insist upon theological agreement as the condition for unity.

The New Testament, on the contrary, has a profound unity coupled with a great diversity of theology. Properly read, I believe that the New Testament is a legacy which will forever suggest how diverging theologies fit the needs of men in differing life situations. And at the same time, as we draw close to the Spirit of that book, we will find ourselves in a unity far more important than agreement in theological thought.

WHERE IS THE UNITY OF THE NEW TESTAMENT?

If we examine the New Testament with care, we can discover a half-dozen to a dozen overlapping layers of theological teaching. But they all witness to the same God and to the same Jesus Christ. The center of the New Testament is God-in-Christ. To quote the apostle Paul, "God was in Christ, reconciling the world to himself." (2 Corinthians 5:19.) (S/R, 19.)

The New Testament is the witness to the new vision of life that became possible to man because Jesus Christ lived among us. What men had found impossible to understand or do before, they were now inspired and motivated to perform. Theology for them meant something more than ideas to talk about; "doing" theology was a way to live.

Very early the church began to preach this new life in Christ. One of the earliest strands of the teaching can be found in the early chapters of the Book of Acts which reports the life of the church in its beginnings. Here is a summary of the main points made by these early preachers:

1. The new age of fulfillment foretold by the prophets has dawned.
2. This has been brought about by God through the ministry, death, and resurrection of Jesus Christ—whom the Scriptures foretold.
3. A new Israel is being formed by God here and now with Jesus as its head. Jesus has been exalted to this place of leadership by God himself, as the Resurrection demonstrated.
4. The new Israel (the church) can testify to a sign of God's presence and glory in the Holy Spirit which has been poured out upon it.
5. The new age will soon reach its fulfillment in the return of Christ in glory.
6. For this reason men must now repent and receive the forgiveness of God and the gift of his Spirit which carries with it the promise of a new life. This new life is called the "life of the age to come."

This is the Christian faith in its earliest form. As it stands here, of course, it is merely like the outline of a sermon or a summary of a short story plot—not very inspiring. But what made it so effective to those who heard and believed it was the new life that was being *demonstrated* by the people of the new faith. They were experiencing the power of the Holy Spirit which pervades the New Testament.

Very early the Christians recognized the Old Testament as an essential part of their own faith. They rejected every effort to make Christianity a religion independent of what God had done for Israel throughout her history. If we look at the faith of the Old Testament, we can see why they felt it to be congenial with their faith. It can be briefly summarized in this way:

1. God, the creator of the world, has graciously revealed himself to man.
2. This revelation included the statement of what is required of man by God and of the blessings of obedience.
3. But man in his weakness and folly refused to respond and obey the divine revelation.
4. The natural consequence of disobedience is punishment—God "judges" mankind and punishes sin.

5. But because God is gracious and loving, his judgment is remedial —God restores and saves in the end, after man repents and turns from his sin.

6. The final salvation designed by God, the state of the individual and of the world, destined to be subject eventually to the divine reign, is to be one of utmost bliss—whether upon this present earth, in a world transformed, or in a golden age to come.*

If we compare these two lists, we see that the New Testament faith is a special variation on the Old Testament faith. The difference is that Jesus Christ is the central figure in God's new graciousness toward men. Even in its variety, the New Testament does not depart from these concepts.

As I have confessed, such outlines do not inspire. They are not meant to inspire but to analyze. They are like the bones of the body—a mere skeleton without flesh. What is the flesh on these theological bones? It is the flesh of a community that lives in the world as God's creation, trusting in his inexhaustible loving-kindness and realizing his guiding presence in everything. Christ is the name for this presence and this love! God demonstrated it through him as he taught and embodied it. And in his fellowship we come to know it as the meaning of our lives. (S/R, 20.)

These summaries are after all merely an analysis of the biblical message in its earliest Christian form. To feel the call of this proclamation, one should hear in his imagination those first apostles preaching with the fire of the Spirit burning in their blood. That would have been inspiring indeed!

■ Let one person be prepared to summarize this entire last section for the group. The lists on pages 39-40 will help to illustrate the unity of the New Testament.

■ Have an oral evaluation of this session. As time permits let persons complete one or the other of these statements:

The most helpful thing that happened to me today was ———————.

Our progress was hindered today when ———————————.

■ Close the session with the benediction "God Be in My Head"

(Resource Packet, item 1). Divide the class into two groups. Let the groups read alternate lines. (It is also printed on page 27 of this book.)

■ Let the leadership team be prepared to give assignments for the next chapter of study and the members of the group be prepared to accept the assignments. See especially page 37.

NOTES ON CHAPTER 2

Page 29: William Law, quoted in Aldous Huxley, *The Perennial Philosophy* (Harper and Row, 1945), pages 196-97.

Pages 39-40: Frederick C. Grant. *An Introduction to New Testament Thought* (Abingdon Press, 1950), pages 14-15. Copyright 1950 by Pierce and Smith. Used by permission.

UNICEF PHOTO BY KEN HEYMAN

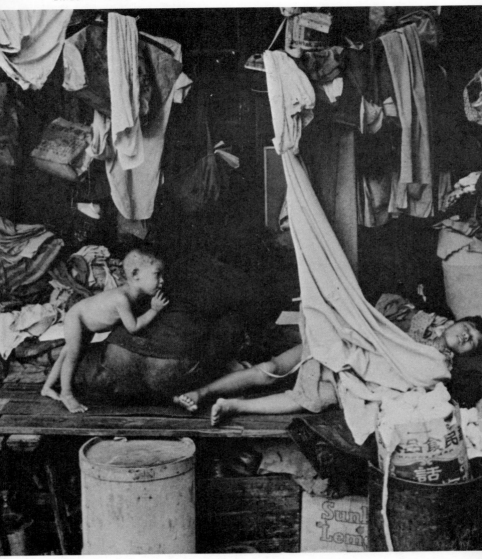

I believe in God the Father Almighty, maker of heaven and earth.

Read these selections in your Bible:
1 Corinthians 8:1-3
The true knowledge is God's knowledge of us.

Ephesians 4:7, 11-14
Unity and maturity in Christ.

2 Timothy 4:1-4
To argue for the truth in Christ.

Acts 15:6-29
The Jerusalem council.

3
□□

BIBLE, CHURCH, AND CREED

"The church is not expected to *proclaim* truths, but *to be* true, to be engaged in the world without compromise and to express its own truthfulness by concrete and practical decisions" (italics added) . [Such faithfulness and sincerity requires a church] "that is not a slave to its own history. We need instead a church that relies on God's grace and wisdom in its weakness and ignorance." *

*   *   *

Have you ever felt that religion would be more appealing if it were not organized? Did it ever seem to you that a great deal of the church seems to be forever bailing, just keeping itself afloat (so to speak) with maintenance activi-

---

■ *As you arrive at your place of meeting, check the assignment chart for specific preparation to be made before the session begins.*

■ *Set goals for your study of this chapter as suggested on page 16.*

ties? I mean raising money, building buildings, conducting evangelistic campaigns for members, and the like.

On the other hand, has the notion ever struck you that our society would be better if everyone had the same religion—our own, of course? We call this a Christian nation. Perhaps the state should see to it that the Christian faith is taught in the schools and supported by taxes!

And what about creeds? Have the various statements of faith bothered you? Honestly now! Have you always found yourself in agreement with the official way of announcing the faith? Do you feel, for example, that literal belief in every part of the Apostles' Creed is the heart of religion? Can one still call himself a Christian if he disagrees with the Apostles' Creed? (S/R, 21.)

These same issues have been a part of the life of faith from the beginning. Much of our history is concerned with them. This and the next chapter are about the struggle of the church to define its faith in terms of organization, its relationship to the state, and the place of official beliefs. Of course, there were other questions that had to be dealt with—and we will touch on them, too, in the proper place. But I want you to realize that in reading about the life of the church from say, A.D. 100 to around 1600—about 1,500 years—you are reading about questions that are still with us today.

Professor Hans Küng, outspoken leader of reform within the Roman Catholic Church and director of the Institute for Ecumenical Research at the University of Tübingen, Germany, addressed himself to the condition of the church. Too often, he suggested, Christians have regarded themselves in possession of truths that must be defended. This has led to a "siege mentality" in the church that locks up its truths and protects itself from the world. (See the quotation by Dr. Küng at the beginning of this chapter.)

■ Look at the questions raised in the third paragraph of this chapter. Let members of the group respond in turn to these questions: Do the questions raised there bother you? Why? How would you answer any or all of them?

Now, let one person read aloud while others follow silently, S/R, 21. Give particular attention to the last paragraph. To grasp the full meaning of the statement beginning "*Anything* else," have members of the group substitute a specific example for each of the phrases. For example, in place of "a particular doctrinal formulation" substitute "the Apostles' Creed."

Discuss: What, then, is essential to the gospel? You might begin by saying what the gospel is not. For example, the gospel is not a particular doctrinal formulation.

■ Prior to this session one or more persons in your group might interview the minister or other representatives of local church groups who visit prospective members. They would ask these representatives: What questions are most often asked by those considering membership in your church? Are they interested in doctrinal beliefs? size of the church? budget? nursery facilities? what? What information do the visitors usually give about your church? Let the interviewers report their findings to the class. Evaluate these in light of S/R, 21.

A BRIEF FORECAST

Most of the New Testament had been written by the end of the first century (A.D. 100). The twenty-seven books had not yet been collected into a single volume, however. In spite of persecution, the church had spread to most of the large cities in the Roman Empire. It had not come to any self-conscious awareness of itself as an enduring organization.

In this early period, little thought had been given to formulating its faith into creedal symbols. Christians hoped they would be left alone by the Roman government so that they might practice their faith without interference.

Within two hundred years (by about A.D. 300), things had changed. Shortly after this date, Constantine, an emperor friendly to the Christian faith, issued an edict that made it possible for Christians to gather for worship and practice their faith without state interference. Long before Constantine's death, it was clear that he wanted to use the church to unify his empire.

In less than another two hundred years, this same empire had collapsed—invaded by barbarian Germanic tribes. For about a thousand years, the church engaged in the task of building the civilization which we call Medieval Christendom.

This long period was concluded with a corruption of the Christian ideals and the coming of the great reformers—Luther, Calvin, Zwingli, and many others. For about a hundred years these reformers worked to formulate a new understanding of the Christian faith. They bequeathed to us the basic beliefs of Protestant Christianity. Then followed a period of deterioration in Protestantism. This period led in England to the evangelical awakening of which John Wesley was a leading figure.

In Roman Catholicism, the corruption in the church led to what is called the Counter Reformation. The pope called the Council of Trent to deal with doctrinal decisions in the Roman church, reform of abuses in the church, and to discuss a new crusade against the Turks. This council began in 1545 and did not end until 1563.

For convenience of reference here is a chart (in round numbers) of the periods just outlined:

4 B.C. to A.D. 100	Jesus and the New Testament Church
A.D. 100 to A.D. 300	Persecution, growth, and consolidation
A.D. 300 to A.D. 500	Official religion of the Roman Empire
A.D. 500 to A.D. 1500	The Middle Ages—Medieval Christendom
A.D. 1500 to A.D. 1600	The Protestant Reformation and the Catholic Counter Reformation

It is obvious that we can only take a few themes from this long period, but we should have this outline in mind to keep ourselves aware of the setting for the issues we will discuss.

■ To refresh your minds about church history, listen again to the recording "The Witnessing Church" (Resource Packet, *We Have This Heritage*, item 5) .

46

DO WE NEED THE BIBLE?

At first, the church was a spontaneous fellowship of people who gathered in homes or in friendly synagogues to hear about and share their faith in Jesus Christ. Most of the stories and sayings about Jesus were carried about in the memories of the people. Some letters, written by Paul and a few others, were saved and passed around to be read in the fellowship meetings. The Old Testament was the Bible of these early Christians, most of whom were Jews.

Inevitably a problem came up that troubled these informal fellowships: conflicting reports were circulated concerning the faith. The reports about Jesus did not always agree and there were even more variations about the meaning of faith. As long as the apostles were living, false reports could be corrected by the eyewitnesses.

Some of these accounts of the sayings of Jesus and accounts of his life were written down. As I have already noted, the letters of Paul had been circulated among the churches. To these letters were now added the accounts of the life and sayings of Jesus. These collections were preserved with special care. Other books and letters not in the New Testament today were also circulated and read in the churches.

Although most of the books in our New Testament were written by A.D. 100, it took several hundred years more to decide which of the many writings should be considered authoritative. The question asked about each book was: Was this book written by an apostle? The apostolic authorship of several books, such as Hebrews and Revelation, was doubted, but these were finally admitted. (Paul was accepted as an apostle.) (S/R, 22.) It was not until the year A.D. 393 that the books today in our New Testament were agreed on as *the* authoritative books for the church.

Many Christians of the twentieth century are unaware of how the New Testament as we have it came into being. From among many writings, some very much like the New Testament as we know it, and some quite different, the twenty-seven books we know were chosen. To understand the New Testament better, we need to know something about the books and writings that were left out and why. There was, for instance, one called "The First Gospel of the Infancy of Jesus Christ." It tells among other things how when the boy Jesus played with his friends he would make clay figures of animals and then would make them come alive so that they would walk. He would make clay birds, and they would fly. (*S/R, 23.*)

■ Let two persons read aloud the two incidents described in *S/R,* 23. This account of the early life of Jesus was circulated in the early church but was not accepted for inclusion in the New Testament. What is the substantial difference between the miracles here and the miracles that are reported in the New Testament? What would you think of Jesus today if these stories were a part of the New Testament? Would the inclusion of such material cause any change in your attitude toward Jesus or the New Testament? Would it strengthen or weaken your faith? Why?

Some of the rejected writings were less fanciful, more philosophical writings. The church felt these books were dangerous to purity of faith. One of them was "The Gospel According to Thomas." The manuscript of this book was found in 1946 in upper Egypt. It contains many sayings found also in the Gospels, and others that are very wise. The tone of the work did not sound apostolic. Scholars now agree and believe this "gospel" belonged to a group called gnostics (pronounced *NOSS-ticks*) .

Gnosticism (pronounced *NOSS-ti-sizm*) was one of the first intellectual religious movements that threatened to confuse Christians about the true meaning of their faith. Instead of putting *faith* at the foundation of Christianity, they put *knowledge.* Agnostic is one who *knows,* from the Greek word *gnosis* (knowledge) . We still use the word *agnostic* (literally, "uncertain of knowing") for one who says that we cannot know whether or not there is a God.

Gnosticism taught that secret knowledge came from special religious practices. They believed that faith was an inferior form of knowledge and the "perfected" ones who had the secret knowledge were superior. This tradition was oriental. It came into Christendom from the East and is kin to certain forms of the Buddhist and Hindu faiths. These latter faiths emphasize salvation through dispelling ignorance rather than through repentance and faith.

The primitive Christian faith taught that men would know God only if they repented of their sins, believed the gospel —the good news of Jesus—and expressed their faith in love. "Faith working through love," to use Paul's expression, was the apostolic way. The way of knowledge through visions and secret teaching, the church pointed out, led to the pride of an intellectual elite rather than to the fellowship of sacrificial love. So the church condemned gnosticism as an error and a threat to the true faith.

There are modern variations of this old gnostic theme. One of them, I think, is the idea that man can be saved through scientific knowledge. What is suggested by this notion is that, as ignorance gives way to more and more knowledge, our problems will melt away. No change in human nature will be required, no repentance, no struggle to live the life of faith and love. But the direction of human affairs seems to point to the fact that with every growth in knowledge there is increasing danger that selfish and fearful men will use it for the destruction of the race rather than its benefit. (*S/R*, 24.)

Another variation of the gnostic theme is the widespread belief that perhaps Christianity is too narrow a way of salvation and that we should take oriental religions—Buddhism and Hinduism particularly—more seriously. Eastern mysticism does not perhaps affect the masses of uneducated Christians, but it has a great appeal to intellectuals. This appeal is understandable because it supports the notion of a spiritual elite which "knows" over against the ignorant masses.

The present flurry of interest in the drug LSD, which induces ecstatic experiences, is a popularized form of gnosticism. Its advocates write about the experiences induced by the drug in somewhat the same way that mystics have written about their own visionary experiences. (S/R, 25.)

The point of this section is that the church needed an authentic standard by which to test the varieties of expressions of the Christian faith; the New Testament became that standard of authority to keep the Christian message true to itself. The church today must turn again and again to the New Testament to test its faith.

> ■ Group discussion: Luther believed in the mediation of the Word; that is, God never speaks to anyone directly but affirms the written and spoken Word in the heart. American revivalism and the circuit riders advocated direct revelation, though Wesley as well as Luther had condemned this idea. What is the attitude of people today toward the place of the Bible? Is it considered a standard and essential source of revelation, or is religious experience the important fact? Give evidence to support your answer.

DO WE NEED A CHURCH?

We have already started the answer to that question. The church first collected the documents of the faith known as the New Testament. Christianity was first a fellowship; the book came later.

Most of us do not object to the *fellowship* idea of the church. What bothers some people is the *organization* of the fellowship. (S/R, 26.)

To see how organization developed, we might study an incident in the early years of the church of Corinth to which Paul wrote several letters. At first a spontaneous fellowship at Corinth was sufficient. But as the fellowship developed, certain strange notions and even stranger activities emerged.

Paul, as the founder of the church, felt it necessary to exert some discipline and to advise the church.

The Corinthians were dividing into separate parties and fighting one another. Their celebration of the Holy Communion was in danger of becoming a kind of spiritual orgy. The so-called "speaking in tongues" was producing chaos and obscuring the meaning of the gospel. It was to these problems that Paul's letters spoke. It took his authority as an apostle to put things right.

The Jerusalem council reported in Acts 15 is another example of how the early church organized to deal with different points of view within the church. It was in response to such problems as those in Corinth that the early churches developed an organization with recognized spiritual leaders such as pastors and bishops. These leaders had the responsibility to keep the fellowship from falling away—sometimes quite innocently and unconsciously—from the original faith.

The church had to struggle to define itself and maintain a witness to the world. Leaders tried to protect the church from alien ideas and practices. As the church dealt with these problems, an authoritative church structure developed to compliment and interpret its authoritative Scripture. Pastors and bishops were given authority to settle many local differences.

■ To gain some understanding of why the church developed an organized structure very early in its life, read 1 Corinthians 11:17-34 or Acts 15:1-35.

Now, suppose your church had no organized structure—no official board, no commissions, no regulations for the operation of your church school, no educational requirements for the clergy— what would your church be like? What problems would you be facing? Give your imagination free rein.

Discuss: What do you, as a church member, consider to be your specific responsibility for the church as an institution?

■ Use the filmslip "The Sun and the Umbrella" (Resource Packet, item 3) to initiate discussion of the problems that exist in relation to the institutional church, the Bible, and creeds. The Leaders'

Guide in the packet includes specific suggestions to guide your discussion.

DO WE NEED CREEDS?

Do you sometimes feel that the creeds you recite in church do not express your true beliefs? Some people even refuse to join in saying a creed or at least keep silent when a phrase is used with which they do not literally agree. Why can't we have our own personal creeds?

These are important questions which point to some very fundamental truths. One of these truths is that each of us must formulate his faith to his own insights. Another is that intellectual integrity is a very precious value.

But I think that our objection to the official creeds of the church needs to be put into its historical setting. To put it in a nutshell—the Christian creeds evolved in conflict with competing religious creeds to make clear just which of them were *not* consistent with the Christian faith.

Take for instance the so-called Apostles' Creed. (Incidentally, it was not developed by the church in its present form until centuries after the time of the apostles.) The first part of this creed says: "I believe in God the Father Almighty, maker of heaven and earth; and in Jesus Christ his only Son our Lord: who was conceived by the Holy Spirit, born of the Virgin Mary, suffered under Pontius Pilate, was crucified, dead, and buried."

Every phrase of this creed was placed there to clarify an important belief in the early Christian church. Some Christians were being taught that Jesus was not the son of the God of the Old Testament but of some distant deity who had no interest in earthly matters. The second phrase answered that objection.

Further, some said that Jesus was not a real man. He was really a god in disguise; he only *appeared* to be a man. If he was a god, he could neither suffer nor die. The creed answered: He was indeed a man who was born like other men, suffered as they do, and died when he was crucified.

The creeds were all formed in this way. They were not final summaries of all the truth of the faith. They were definitions which were useful at the time to avoid serious mistakes in belief which would pervert the Christian way. Creeds, like the New Testament and the church organization, were practical instruments for letting the faith evolve in a way true to itself.

The development of creeds was in some ways like the development of the Bill of Rights in the United States Constitution. Each of these articles of the Bill of Rights was directed against a specific form of tyranny with which the founding fathers were familiar. The list was not a final complete catalog of all human rights. In fact, other rights have evolved in new circumstances. For instance, we now believe that every American child has a right to an education at public expense at least up through high school. The founding fathers could not have conceived of such a "right" because the circumstances of early American history were so different from circumstances today.

Just as we have an evolving sense of human rights as circumstances unfold, so we have evolving expressions of how we understand the Christian faith. And just as the "right" to an education is an extension of and in harmony with the original constitutional idea of rights, new formulations of the Christian faith have developed in the spirit of the original faith.

At the present time, new creeds are written nearly every time two Christian denominations join. Each has its own way of affirming the faith derived from its own history. The union requires that they come to an understanding in terms of a new statement. (*S/R*, 27.)

At the General Conference in 1966, a request was approved to ask the first General Conference of The United Methodist Church in 1968 to appoint a commission to formulate a new confession of faith. This new doctrinal standard is to be based on the Wesleyan heritage. The commission is to make regular reports to the General Conference.

Formulating a new confession will be an exacting responsibility. Once it is formulated, an even more difficult task will probably be to guide it through to approval by a large General Conference. The major question is this: To what degree should Methodists living today be bound by the doctrinal formulations of the past, including those of John Wesley?

The fact that creed-making must continue, however, also suggests a warning. A new creed should not be an accommodation to the non-Christian way of the world. It should be a clarification of the faith over against those elements in civilization that need to be challenged by the faith. And there is no way to anticipate this centuries in advance. We must trust each generation of living Christians to find the true center of meaning in Christ and express it faithfully.

At least for me, this is an answer to the repetition of some phrases of ancient creeds that no longer seem just exactly right. I am willing to recite them in church as memorials of the church through the ages. They express the solidarity of our fellowship across the centuries. They are not meant to be a final summary, for no creed formulated by men has ever or will ever encompass all of the good news.

■ Group discussion: Why does The United Methodist Church need a creed of its own? Why not just accept the Apostles' Creed or the Nicene Creed? What is unhistorical about appointing a commission to write a creed? How does the writing of this new creed relate to this book's assertion of the recurring need to restate the faith? Where does data on which to base a new creed come from? from the Bible? from tradition? What happens to any creed that is replaced by a newer version? After the Council of Nicaea (A.D. 325), everyone had to give public assent to the Nicene Creed whether he understood it or not. Do we have to believe the Nicene Creed? If not, must we believe the Apostles' Creed? Why? Why not? Can a creed have any real significance in a non-creedal church that presupposes and encourages diversity of beliefs?

WHAT DOES THIS MEAN TO US TODAY?

The Scripture, church, and creed may have preserved the faith; well and good, you may say. But what possible significance has this for us? The original faith is kept from adulteration through the centuries—so what?

A good question. Purity of faith is not an end in itself. The rigid spirit of orthodoxy—"correct opinion"—may be a barrier to spiritual growth. (S/R, 28.)

The only reason for preserving the original faith is the claim that it offers to man something no other way of life can offer. We cannot prove that by argument. However, this claim deserves a fair test. And the only way it can be tested is to try it in reasonably pure form.

Suppose the gnostics had succeeded in adapting Christianity to their views. We cannot honestly say what the result would have been. Probably Christianity would have become something like Buddhism or Hinduism. If someone thinks that would have been good, then he should embrace those faiths rather than Christianity and let the gospel have its own chance.

To be more specific, if the gnostic influence had prevailed, Christianity probably would have rejected Judaism completely and dropped the Old Testament, regarding it as an unworthy religious guide. It would have taught us to despise the world as the creation of an inferior deity. Instead of the spiritual life being a case of "faith working through love," it would have become a series of spiritual practices leading to ecstatic states of consciousness. The great prophetic messages about earthly justice and the struggle to express love in an ever-widening range of social institutions would not have emerged.

Even our own attitudes toward our bodies and ourselves as persons would have been different since the body would then have been thought of as a low and earthy object of no importance to God. And personality, instead of being a value to perfect and mature, would have been something to transcend in a spiritual experience of melting or merging into some transcendental reality.

Of course, none of this is proof. There are those who think that this would have been good. The only proofs we have are these vital experiments in living, and I for one think that the Christian experiment is worth trying. Let others take different paths as they feel they are called.

■ A part of the meaning of "doing theology" is the thinking through and the expressing of faith by each person according to his insights, understanding, and vocabulary.

An additional session may be planned to give opportunity for persons to practice this thinking and expressing. Provide each person with paper and pencil and a copy of the various creeds. These are found in *The Methodist Hymnal* and *The Book of Worship*. Each person may select one creed and study it carefully. Then he may write his understanding of each declaration in the creed and the implications of his understanding for his living. In the light of the development of creeds what should be your attitude toward the rights of persons to express doubts? You might begin your writing like this: "I believe in God the Father Almighty, maker of heaven and earth," means —————————————————————

After a sufficient amount of time for thinking and writing, let persons who worked on particular creeds form discussion groups. If all members studied the same creed, the entire group may share in the same discussion. Go through the creed together taking time for each person to share his understandings of each declaration and the implications of his understanding for daily living.

Discuss: Have persons in the group detected any change in their understanding of the Christian faith since the time they joined the church? What change in understanding has helped persons move toward a mature faith? What change has hindered growth toward a mature faith? Would you say that something is wrong if one's faith has not changed? Why? Why not? How would you describe an effective faith?

■ Take time for evaluation. How would you evaluate this session in terms of your goals? What decisions have you moved toward? What changes have taken place?

■ Close the session with the benediction "God Be in My Head" (Resource Packet, item 1) . (See also page 27 of this book.)

■ Let the leadership team be prepared to give assignments for the next chapter of study and the members of the group be prepared to accept the assignments.

NOTES ON CHAPTER 3

Page 44: From a report on Professor Hans Küng's addresses at the anniversary of the Pacific School of Religion in Berkeley, California, 1966.

CHRIST MOCKED, BY EDOUARD MANET, COURTESY OF THE ART INSTITUTE OF CHICAGO

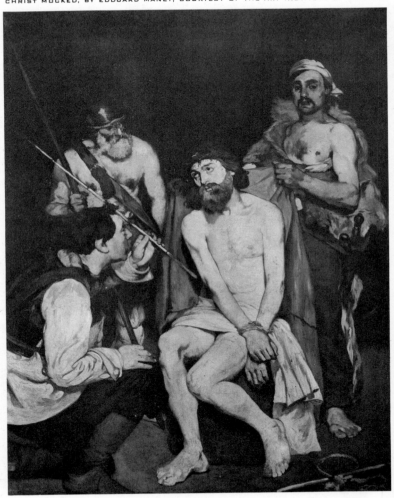

It is comparatively easy to silence people we do not want to hear by calling them heretics or traitors.

Read these selections in your Bible:
Romans 8
Paul describes life in the Spirit.

Galatians 3:1-9
Paul opposes the Spirit to religious legalism.

4

□□□

EVERY MAN A PRIEST

"For freedom Christ has set us free; stand fast therefore, and do not submit again to a yoke of slavery." (Galatians 5:1.)

"Let every person be subject to the governing authorities. For there is no authority except from God, and those that exist have been instituted by God." (Romans 13:1.)

*   *   *

Thus far we have considered the problems that the faith had during its early period before becoming the official religion of an empire. We have seen why the original spontaneous fellowship of the faithful evolved a church organization, a sacred book, and a collection of creeds. We turn first

■ _As you arrive at your place of meeting, check the assignment chart for specific preparation to be made before the session begins._
■ _Set goals for your study of this chapter as suggested on page 16._

to the new problems that faced the faith during the millennium in which it was the dominant religion of Europe and then to a consideration of the Reformation. Then we shall discuss the religious teachings of the reformers.

During about twelve hundred years (from about A.D. 300 to A.D. 1500), the government supported the Catholic faith, or, at times, the church controlled the government. One of the great new ideas coming out of the Reformation was the priesthood of all believers. But this belief did not mean each person was free to follow his conscience on religious matters, even in the Lutheran countries. In 1555, after several years of conflict between Lutherans and Catholics, it was decided that each German prince should decide between the old religion and Lutheranism. If he was a Lutheran, all the people in his territory would have to be Lutherans. If they wanted to keep the old religion, they would have to leave and go to the territory of a Catholic prince.

Religious toleration was not allowed by the reformers. If Catholics were in control of the government, they persecuted Protestants. If Protestants were in control, they persecuted Catholics. Both Catholics and Protestants persecuted others who would not conform.

After the Reformation had been under way for several years, many people felt it was not radical enough. They wanted revolution, not reform. These people withdrew from the newer reforming churches and established congregations of their own. They invited converts to join them. Because in that day, every baby was baptized as soon as possible after birth, these radical Christians demanded that all their converts be rebaptized. They were called the Anabaptists because they felt adults should be baptized again when they were converted. As a by-product of this belief, they stopped baptizing their children.

When these radicals stopped baptizing their children, the

reformers thought they had gone too far. In Switzerland, the reformers persuaded the government to order these people to either have their infants baptized or leave the territory. Many left rather than submit. As this group, the radicals or Anabaptists, won new converts, the reformers became more and more concerned. The government made it illegal to be an Anabaptist and decreed the penalty of death. The mode of capital punishment was ironic; all Anabaptists (who believed in adult baptism only) would be killed by drowning. Several were caught, tied with ropes, and thrown into lakes and rivers.

Where is the priesthood of believers in this sad story? It should be noted that the *church* did not kill these people. They only persuaded the government to do it. The relationship of religion to government has a long history.

■ Begin this session by having members of the group share ideas or questions from their study of this chapter. The subheads from the chapter may be written on chalkboard or newsprint to help persons recall the major ideas.

You may wish to consider some of these questions briefly: What, in your opinion, is the proper relationship between church and state? How much is nonconformity on popular political and religious questions tolerated in your community? Could a Jew or a Unitarian be elected as representative to Congress? What happens when religious terminology is invoked to handle political situations? For example, in relation to family planning or the war in Vietnam? What are the boundaries of individual freedom in the political as well as the religious realm?

THE CASE OF CONSTANTINE

The Emperor Constantine allowed toleration of Christianity in the Roman Empire in A.D. 312, and the fortunes of Christianity changed from that of a persecuted faith to an official religion. No doubt the emperor, with political affairs foremost in his mind, looked upon the church as a means of unifying his empire.

When the churches were caught in an internal struggle

61

over a new heresy sparked by a man named Arius (pronounced *AIR-e-us*), Constantine moved swiftly to bring it to
an end. He called a council of the church at the Greek city of
Nicaea (*ny-SEE-ah*) in 325. He demanded a settlement of the
quarrel. What finally emerged was a denunciation of Arius
and his views and the formulation of one of the great ancient
creeds of the church—the Nicene Creed. (*S/R*, 29.)

When we read this creed, the first thing that strikes us is
that it has a different tone than the Apostles' Creed. The
latter has a *historical* flavor, that is, it refers, at least in part
to historical events—the birth, crucifixion, and burial of
Jesus. The Nicene Creed is *metaphysical* in tone. By this I
mean that it uses concepts from Greek philosophy to express
the faith. Take such a phrase as *of one substance with the
Father*. The Greek word *substance* means that which "stands
under" all appearances ("stance" equals stand; "sub" equals
under). That means that Jesus shared the same essence or
nature as God while having the characteristics of man.

This creed stated Christian belief in the language of the
philosophy of that day. Such a Greek restatement was necessary because it took place in a culture dominated by Greek
ideas. To the church, the Nicene Creed was another successful redefinition of the faith. To Constantine, no doubt, it was
a smart political move. The empire now had one official
religion.

First, let us take the positive side of this relationship between the church and state. With the political power behind
it, the church could expand into a mighty institution that
was later strong enough to hold civilization together when
the empire finally collapsed.

It forced churchmen to ask a whole new set of questions.
These questions arose because the church was now responsible for civilized life. The church had to ask what kind
of laws were really expressive of the Christian faith: what

62

kind of education, what kind of economic system, what kind of family life, what kind of political system?

The result of these labors was what we have called Christendom—the whole body of institutions, laws, practices, and arts that expressed at least for a time, in a specific setting, what it would mean to be a Christian in society. Today we are the heirs of this effort to create a Christian society, though it is a seriously disrupted heritage. (S/R, 30 and 31.)

But this attempt of the church to control society also had a negative side. We can put it in the form of questions: Should political power ever be used to insure religious conformity? Should the state officially embrace one form of faith? Should citizens who do not agree with the majority or the official faith be refused the right to exercise full citizenship? And from the church point of view: Should persons who are not properly religious be denied political office?

If we answer "yes" to all these questions, we seem to be caught in agreement with some very unpleasant facts of history. The "Christian" state did in fact persecute—even torture and kill—citizens who were not orthodox in their beliefs. The so-called "Holy Office" of the church could call upon the sword of the state to destroy unbelievers of all kinds.

Another side-effect of saying "yes" to these questions was that it was easy to agree to Christian beliefs in public. It was tempting for men to accept an easy official belief and enjoy the privileges and power that such orthodoxy conferred upon them. Men grew fat and slack in their faith. After all, it is comparatively easy to silence people we do not want to hear by calling them heretics or traitors, and let the government deal with them.

One of the reasons Luther was successful in his reforms was because the power of the Holy Roman Empire in Germany was divided among the German princes and the emperor needed their support. Luther was protected by his German prince who had economic and political, as well as religious, reasons for not turning him over to the Catholic emperor who would have certainly put him to death.

■ Discuss in the total group: What new questions is the church being forced to ask as a responsible critic of conditions in today's society? What are sources or concerns in society that give rise to these questions? What responsibility does the church as an institution have for these situations in society?

Listen as one person reads aloud S/R, 31. Have a simulated debate. Let one half of the class defend the position set forth in the reading. The other half will oppose the views in the reading. Give evidence to support or refute the idea that "changed men and women" (Christians) would in time change society. When do we say "the church" is acting? When individuals or groups, influenced by the teachings of the church, act or speak out in behalf of equality of opportunity for all races? or of guaranteed income for the poor? or on the other hand, in behalf of the primacy of private property over needs of human beings? Or when?

CAN A SOCIETY ALLOW DISSENT IN RELIGION?

Today we think that a society can allow dissent in religion, but we should not forget how new this idea is. Even the Protestant princes of Germany did not allow Catholics freedom of their faith for many years. Americans often do not realize that this freedom was won only gradually here and in England.

Because it is new, we are not entirely convinced of it ourselves. We are often prone to attack critics of our faith rather than show how they are wrong. This is especially true in the field of political orthodoxy, which, incidentally, has become a kind of religion for many Americans. The worst thing we can say about a person with whom we disagree today is that he is "un-American." A public reputation for being "un-American" will bring all sorts of community pressures on a person, from being socially snubbed to losing his job or his customers.

Does the fact have any significance that being "un-American" seems worse to most of us than being "un-Christian"? We would probably not approve of punishing a person who was not Christian. Why do we often approve punishment of people whom we think are "un-American"? Is it that perhaps Americanism has become for many of us the center of our faith? (S/R, 32.) Does this, rather than Christ, give the central meaning to our lives?

> ■ Using S/R, 32 as a basis, let four persons, prepared in advance, form a panel to discuss these questions: What is the significance of the fact that being "un-American" seems worse to most of us than being "un-Christian"? What evidence is there that Americanism rather than Christ has become for many of us the center of our faith?
> Allow time for questions and discussion from other members of the group.

The reason for raising this point is simple. It gives us more sympathy for our ancestors who persecuted heretics. In those days, a rejection of the orthodox Christian faith seemed to be a threat against the entire social order, just as today communism seems subversive of our political and economic order. If we want to know to what degree the power of society should be used to shut off those who are not orthodox, we can examine our attitudes toward those today who express unorthodox views in politics and economics rather than in religion. Americans do not feel threatened today by religious heretics, but our society is very concerned about heretics in politics and economics. (S/R, 33.) The church in the past regarded religious heretics with the same fear and disgust many Americans feel toward these political and economic heresies.

Whatever your thought on these matters, one thing seems pretty clear: enforcing religious conformity is bad. The long-run effect of such enforcement is to weaken the quality of religious faith. It silences criticism, and this leads to corruption in the church. It makes orthodoxy profitable, and that leads to hypocrisy. It leaves standard opinions unchallenged, and that leads to thoughtless complacency. It would seem that truth is not something that can be guaranteed by the state. It has to be won over again by real effort in each generation.

■ Let groups of four to six persons select for discussion one of the three parallel sentences (silence/corruption; orthodoxy/hypocrisy; unchallenged opinions/complacency) in the above paragraph. More than one group may deal with the same sentence.

Do you agree with the premise of the first part of the sentence? What evidence can you cite to support your view, to validate the sentence? Does the conclusion of the second part of the sentence necessarily follow the first part? What else may follow when the situation of the first part of the sentence exists?

During the early years of the period we are now thinking about, faith was growing spontaneously all over Europe. As the social life of the Roman Empire fell into decay, thousands of men and women went into the church as the only vital social organization. Later, religious orders sprang up on all sides; great cathedrals were built; and wonderful works of art flourished. Better than that, a great many truly saintly persons, willing to give their all for the faith, emerged in every corner of Europe. I mean such people as St. Francis of Assisi, St. Catherine of Siena, St. John of the Cross, and St. Theresa.

But when this great impulse had spent itself and the work of construction was completed, the real evils of a state religion began to show themselves. These evils all sprang from the suppression of great religious figures who desired to reform the system. Savonarola, an Italian monk, called for changes in the church and was burned publicly at the stake after prolonged torture. There were hundreds like him. It was only the special political circumstances of northern Europe and Switzerland that the great Protestant reformers did not meet a like fate.

66

THE AMERICAN EXPERIMENT

America is now engaged in an experiment of great importance. This experiment is the attempt to build a democratic society composed of many different religious, ethnic, and racial groups. It is not easy. Every society depends upon a certain broad agreement upon fundamental values. Can we create and maintain that agreement in the midst of our diversities? If we succeed, we will have one of the richest and most varied cultures in human history. (S/R, 34.)

But what does this suggest about the Christian claim to have the true way for all men? I think that it means that we must forget the hope of ever enforcing this belief. We must return to the methods of the early church and win the world by the power of the gospel itself. Theologically, this means we recognize that true faith must be embraced freely by free men. It means that we can never rest content with large public acceptance, but must win each new generation by the freshness with which we present the gospel. Education must be enlarged to acquaint each new generation with the treasures of faith, and compassionate, intelligent evangelism must completely displace all forms of social pressure.

Does this seem impractical? It seems to have been God's way when he sent a Nazarene carpenter without any trappings of prestige or power to be the symbol of his presence in history. The medieval ideal of a Christian culture is still valid—but the means must now be different. We can never hope again for another Constantine. We should not want another. Only when a person can dissent without fear of persecution can the ideas of the Christian faith be accepted for their own worth.

■ Some understanding of the diversity of views existing in society may be gained by having members of the group brainstorm (list without discussion) responses to this question: What, in my thinking, are the fundamental values upon which a society is built? Have

67

one person write the responses on chalkboard or newsprint as they are given.

On the basis of the responses to the question discussed: Where are some possible points of agreement between church and state?

Now read *S/R, 34*. Do you agree or disagree with the ruling of the Kansas Supreme Court against the Amish father? Why?

■ Discuss as a group: What is your understanding of the idea that Christians must forget the hope of *enforcing* the claim that Christianity is the true way for all men?

Then let three persons, prepared in advance, present the playlet "The Convert" (Resource Packet, item 4). See the Leaders' Guide in the packet for detailed instructions.

Discuss: Suppose you were faced with a situation similar to the one in the playlet, how would you react? Is it possible for a Christian to take the attitude that any religion that satisfies a person is right for that person? Why, in your understanding, is Christianity the superior (that is, the best but not the only) religion? Or the only valid religion for you?

In a culture where many religions are held valid or where many religions are respected, what is the best way to witness to your faith?

THE AGE OF REFORM

Just about the time that Columbus discovered America, Europe was on the verge of what we call the Protestant Reformation. Why did the reformers cause such a stir? And, most important, what does their reform mean to us?

Some of the immediate effects of the reform were pretty bad. Christendom was split into two Christian camps— Protestant and Roman Catholic. The Christian message was to that degree damaged. Today, for instance, many missionaries are faced by their listeners with the question, "Which Christianity is the true one?" And many non-Christians will not even seriously consider the Christian claim because of this bitter rivalry among the faithful.

This split had terrible human consequences in the century that followed the reform. From 1618 to 1648 the so-called Thirty Years' War raged between Catholics and Protestants in Europe. Millions were slaughtered. When peace came, it was not a victory for either side. It was a peace of exhaustion.

Christendom has never fully recovered from the supicions and the damage of these wars of religion.

On the positive side of the ledger, we may put the new clarification of the faith that emerged in the Reformation. One of the reasons for the vigor of present-day theology is the revival of the teachings of that period. The violence of the time obscured some of the great achievements. Perhaps only today can they be made clear. Even the Roman Catholic Church seems in a mood to consider the real meaning of the Reformation instead of denouncing it as the work of antichrist (just as Protestants had called the pope antichrist). Luther's great hymn "A Mighty Fortress Is Our God" now appears in Catholic hymnals.

One way we can assess this achievement is to examine briefly the main elements of the Reformation teaching.

WHAT IS PROTESTANTISM?

Most Protestants have only the haziest idea of what distinguishes their faith from that of Roman Catholic Christians. What views they have of the matter have about as much relation to the facts as a cartoon picture of the American president has to his actual appearance. The features are distorted according to the political opinions of the cartoonist.

Looking back upon the Catholic Church of the Middle Ages through the eyes of the reformers we tend to see only corruption, and this is not entirely fair. Of course, there was corruption. The Reformation was necessary. It focused the faith in a new image of self-understanding. It is to this new focus that we must now turn.

What is Protestantism? Let me start by pointing out that it cannot be finally defined, because part of its spirit is that of continuous change, endless reformation. Perhaps the best we can do is to indicate a large number of convictions shared by Protestants. In this brief summary Robert McAfee

Brown's *The Spirit of Protestantism* (Oxford University Press, 1961) is a guide. Here are some of the central shared beliefs.

THE CENTRALITY OF GRACE AND THE LIFE OF FAITH

The crisis of Protestantism arose, at least for Luther, in a struggle with guilt. In searching for peace with God, he tried the various practices of his church and found them wanting. What released him was the realization that the God revealed in Jesus was a gracious God, rather than a severe judge who tallied up good and bad deeds. He came to believe through his study of the Scriptures that God was a God of grace. Grace means that God has accepted us in spite of our sins and failures and secured for us a loving relationship to him. He came to us in Jesus Christ to let us know that our relationship to him is not based upon some merit system, but upon his unlimited love. This is the meaning of Paul's remark that this happened "while we were yet sinners."

The old way of understanding was that God would accept me only after I had proved myself by the cultivation of appropriate virtues. God commands us to "be perfect," but it is apparent that this is really not possible. After we have tried our hardest, we still fall short of that mark. The result is despair. If we imagine that we have succeeded, we fall into self-deception and pride.

The new way of grace says that we are accepted by God just as we are—"while we were yet sinners." The virtuous life follows from this joyful sense of God's forgiveness and acceptance. Grace empowers us to live a life that we could not have lived by our own efforts.

Of course, this is not a "one-shot" affair. We need the grace of acceptance and the help of the Spirit all along the way. But the true beginning comes with the acceptance of the grace of our Lord Jesus Christ. The good life follows rather than precedes it.

This is briefly what Luther meant by "faith alone" or "grace alone." He wanted to turn men away from the futile and discouraging effort to make themselves presentable to God by their own proud efforts. Here is a sentence from Luther that is worth remembering: "Faith is a lively, reckless confidence in the grace of God."

THE AUTHORITY OF SCRIPTURE

Just as the reformers cried "faith alone," they also cried "Scripture alone." This attitude toward the Bible challenged the whole authoritative structure of the medieval church with the pope at its head. The Roman Church claimed that the authority for the spiritual life rested in the duly constituted church officials. It was their right to interpret the Scriptures as well.

Protestantism gave the Bible to the people and asked them to trust the plain word of the Scriptures interpreted by a Spirit-enlightened conscience. As they read their Bibles, it seemed to them that the church of the sixteenth century had become something vastly different from the church of the New Testament. This new attitude led to a conviction that vast reforms of the organization of the church were needed —the greatest need was to reject the Roman bishop's authority (the pope's) over all Christians. Luther was put out of the Catholic Church because he rejected the authority of the pope and church councils. (S/R, 35.)

Among the reformers difficulties developed which we can appreciate today. The Bible is not as plain as it might have seemed. Not long after the onset of the Reformation, Protestants found difficulties in agreeing. From that time forward, they began to split into different groups, each claiming to have the right interpretation. We know that in many if not

71

most cases this splitting reflected social and cultural differences rather than religious beliefs alone. But since there was no arching authority, such as the pope in the Catholic Church, to unify interpretations, this splintering went on (and goes on) endlessly. This has been one of Protestantism's chief problems.

What is the answer to this? We are struggling today to find it. The answer has many parts. One is a careful reconsideration of the true authority of the Bible. Does it lie in the printed word? Or does it lie in the Lord who speaks through the Book? Another part of the answer is to reconsider the role of the church, as the body of faithful believers, in the interpretation of the Bible.

This is an answer, in part, to the question, How does God speak through the Bible? Certainly we know that he does not speak to just anyone who reads it. The skeptic who reads it to debunk it is not likely to hear the Word. The man who reads it as enjoyable literature does not hear the Word. Who hears the Word? Only a faithful listening community of faithful people. And this is a good definition of the true church.

THE SOVEREIGNTY OF GOD

To believe in the sovereignty of God means to trust in the sureness of his love, to know that nothing in creation can stand in the way of his intention for us—with the possible exception of our own refusal of that love.

This faith means, in Paul's words, that nothing in "all creation, will be able to separate us from the love of God in Christ Jesus our Lord." (Romans 8:39.)

This doctrine can be a great comfort to us in times of trouble. The Reformers were often persecuted to the edge of despair. They encouraged themselves by singing such songs as this:

> . . . The Lord our God is good;
> His mercy is forever sure;
> His truth at all times firmly stood,
> And shall from age to age endure.
> —*The Methodist Hymnal*, 21.

THE PRIESTHOOD OF ALL BELIEVERS

This doctrine is a natural consequence of the beliefs we have already outlined. It is on the priesthood of Christ that the New Testament church was founded. Christ's priesthood was shown in the bearing of the burdens of others. The medieval church had said priests and other persons who had committed their lives to the church were the first-class Christians. All others were second-class. The Protestant reformers said this was not true; all men were priests. No group or person—whether ordained or not—had special status with God. The priesthood (or servanthood) of the Christian did *not* mean "every man his *own* priest," but "every man a priest to his neighbor." We are to pray for others, to sacrifice ourselves to God if necessary on behalf of others. (*S/R, 36* and *37*.) Luther believed every person should be a Christ to his neighbor; this is the meaning of the priesthood of believers.

We cannot leave to the clergy the work of reading, studying, praying, listening, and obeying through which the Word is spoken to mankind. That is a job for all of us.

■ Form work groups of four to six persons. Each group may proceed in this fashion:

a. Each person will read silently the preceding discussion of the priesthood (servanthood) of all believers.

b. As a group study the pictures in the Bulletin Board Display I (Resource Packet, item 2). Directions for assembling the bulletin board display are in the Leaders' Guide in the packet.

c. Discuss: In what sense can the priesthood (servanthood) of all believers actually be practiced in a person's life? What are some situations when we can be agents of reconciliation or redemption?

d. Study the Scripture mentioned on the bulletin board and *S/R,* 36 and 37. What do these readings suggest to you about the role of a priest (servant)? Make a list of other words (nouns) that name a way you might perform the role of a priest (servant). For example, listener, comforter, and so forth.

e. Discuss: What do you see as the responsibility of the entire local congregation acting as priest (as servant)? In which of these responsibilities are you willing to participate as a member?

If time allows, one person from each group may report to the entire group.

CONCLUSION

We have traced some of the theological issues facing Christians through fifteen hundred years of history. It is obviously too brief a treatment. But it has been my intention to show that the issues which Christians struggled with during those years still have an importance for us today.

We cannot ignore the truth about the faith which they uncovered in their struggles to be faithful to the original gospel. We can see their failures—glaring failures—but we can also see their monumental achievements.

When Martin Luther died, one of his closest friends wrote in his diary a simple account of Luther's death. After relating the event in a matter-of-fact way, the friend added, "And though he be dead—he lives!"

The spirit of the great figures of the Reformation lives on wherever the church tries to be faithful to the living God and to renew itself to meet the needs of the present day.

The "principle of Protestantism" is that God reveals himself in every age, and that each generation must continue the Reformation with specific patterns for renewal and reform. (S/R, 38.) We must take upon ourselves the burden of reinterpretation of the will of God and application of it in our own time.

■ Use S/R, 121 to help you evaluate the life and growth of your group. You may wish to have persons mark the chart individually then discuss the items as a group. What does the doctrine of the priesthood of all believers have to say to the atmosphere, the attitude, and the accomplishments of your group?

74

■ Pray together as a benediction "God Be in My Head" (Resource Packet, item 1).

■ Let the leadership team be prepared to give assignments for the next chapter of study and the members of the group be prepared to accept the assignments. See especially page 83.

EWING GALLOWAY

What god am I worshiping right now?

Read these selections in your Bible:
Psalms 103:1-5
God brings fullness of being to men.

Psalms 104:1-4
The greatness of God seen in nature.

1 John 4:7-8, 12, 16, 19-21
The great truth: God is known through love.

5

□□

GOD

"If we were concerned with knowledge of determinate facts, faith might be written off as belief without sufficient grounds. But in the realm of existence, faith seems to be a distinguishing mark of humanity at its growing best. For faith is man's unfailing contact with Reality even when his own powers fail. It is the experience of meaning when every evidence testifies to meaninglessness, the rising hope that even in failure a new life awaits one in the coming hour. Faith is the power to sense the awe in things when they have become dull and commonplace, the light that shines in events when our eyes have become tired with watching. Faith awakens the warmth of forgiveness when we have grown cold with bitterness and hurt, and arouses love for someone

■ *As you arrive at your place of meeting, check the assignment chart for specific preparation to be made before the session begins.*
■ *Set goals for your study of this chapter as suggested on page 16.*

whom all observations have disclosed as unlovable. Faith can transfigure human sorrow and irreplaceable loss with the certainty of joy and hope. It can assure of Reality's acceptance and healing when one is sick with moral failure and seemingly impregnable self-concern. This same faith can cast a man into despair about himself when he is proud and self-sufficient, and bring him out of his despair into humble self-acceptance. Faith can illuminate the way one must take when the light of experience and thought has grown dim. Faith is the absolute assurance that nothing, absolutely nothing in all creation, can separate us from the Holy Love which we but dimly see and but haltingly grope after. Faith, thus understood, is God's grip on man, the power of the Hand that cannot be loosed, the Life that is everlasting." *

*   *   *

A wit once defined God as "an oblong blur." Perhaps you have felt that the whole idea of God in a lot of religious talk was pretty fuzzy. If someone asks me whether I believe in God, I am inclined to ask them, "What God?" The reason for this is that often another person's idea of God is miles away from my own.

THE CHRISTIAN IDEA OF GOD

Let us start then with this understanding: the God we are talking about is the Christian God, the Being whom the New Testament calls the "Father of our Lord Jesus Christ." It seems to me that the Christian God can best be thought of as creative, sovereign, holy love.

God is *creative*. The Bible begins with God creating the world. As the story unfolds, it is clear that he is not finished with his creation. In the world he continues creatively leading it toward his purposes with loving care. The religious word for this care is *providence*. Providence does not mean

78

that God "provides" merely in a physical sense. It means that he is creatively at work, bringing his world nearer to his final purposes. (*S/R,* 39.) And we must remember that he is still at it. As Jesus said, "My Father is working still, and I am working." (John 5:17.) This statement plainly says that God will continue his work.

God is *sovereign.* We speak of sovereign states or sovereign countries. By this we mean that these powers are not subject to the will of any political power outside themselves. When we speak of God as sovereign, we are trying to say that he is completely the master—the sovereign—of his creation. This mastery is sometimes hard to believe when we see the way in which his will is contradicted in human affairs.

God is *holy.* Holiness suggests the majesty and glory of God, the deep mystery we can never completely understand. Holiness implies wholeness. We speak of a man of character as having integrity. This last word comes from the same root as the word *integer* which means "one." We mean that he is not double-minded, or double-tongued. He is what he appears to be. The holiness of God is his absolute trustworthiness and goodness. He is thus the measure of all human integrity and all human goodness.

God is *love.* The New Testament word is *agape* (pronounced *ah-GAH-pay*) . There are, of course, many kinds of love. Here we are talking about the kind of love that we want to attribute to God. (See the Bible readings at the beginning of this chapter.)

The New Testament uses this word *agape* when speaking about the special kind of love God has for us. When I use the word *love* in this chapter, it is God's love I have in mind. This love is different from romantic love or friendship, or an attraction to things that we "love," like baseball or music. (*S/R,* 40.) This love is completely self-giving love which flows out and over all creation without limit. It does not hold itself back from evil men. Nor does it judge any human being so disgusting that it does not flow endlessly toward him. There is no racial or class membership, no kind of belief, no kind of act that makes God withhold his love from men. Jesus said simply, God sends his sunlight and rain "on the just and on the unjust" alike. (Matthew 5:45.) Paul saw in Jesus this love of God and said, "While we were yet sinners Christ died for us." (Romans 5:8.)

Because this love is also creative, sovereign, and holy, it redeems those whom it touches. It restores them, making them into beings who are worthy of love.

Now that we understand the God we are talking about, let us turn to some other questions.

■ Let one person be prepared to review quickly the Christian idea of God discussed above. A simple outline of four main points and two or three subpoints may be prepared in advance to guide the presentation.

Discuss: Why do we feel it necessary to find some kind of formula for expressing a truth (for example, God)? Why do persons strive so hard to maintain conformity to a formula? Some persons believe that God can be contained in a formula. What may happen to their faith when they encounter a new idea of God? What can you say about God after reading S/R, 39 and 1 John 4:7-8, 12, 16, 19-21?

Read S/R, 41. Why do some Christians feel they must protect the message of the gospel from the power of the world?

WHAT DOES IT MEAN TO HAVE A GOD?

A "god" is the object of one's worship. It is whoever or whatever a person believes worthy of highest adoration and final obedience. Martin Luther once said, "Trust and faith of the heart alone make both God and idol. . . . For the two, faith and God, hold close together. Whatever then thy heart clings to . . . and relies upon, that is properly thy God." *

To have a "god" is not to have certain notions in your head —it is to orient your whole life toward the values and meanings that your "god" symbolizes. In the Christian faith, this is the God of sovereign, creative, and holy love.

80

The center of loyalty of man's life determines the kind of man he will be. If he is, for instance, centered in himself or in his group, he will treat all others as outsiders unworthy of his concern.

The central loyalty of a *group* determines the kind of group it will be. A nation, for instance, dedicated to the freedom and worth of persons, will be very different from one dedicated to the supremacy of, say, German or American culture, or the white race. As the Bible says, righteousness exalts a nation (Proverbs 14:34) and wickedness degrades it.

One of the ways theology witnesses to the gospel is to make clear which God we profess to have as our God, both as persons and as a "Christian nation."

HOW DO WE KNOW THERE IS A GOD?

The question is often asked. But it is the wrong question. A better question would be: What god am I presently worshiping? The answer to that can only be found by asking one or two other questions: (1) What, for me, is ultimately worthwhile? Or (2) what power do I really trust in life? If we will answer these two questions, we will know who or what our god is.

But once we know that, would we then ask about such a "god's" existence? I think not. The existence of the god men actually worship is not in doubt. All of us know that something or someone is ultimately worthwhile; all of us really trust some power. It is evident, therefore, that a god exists for us.

Perhaps the reason we ask about God's existence is that we do not truly worship or trust him. Perhaps another reason for raising the question is that other men who do not believe ask it. The Scripture tells us that we should always be ready to give an account of the faith that is in us. But I think we should realize that arguments do not convert anyone—not even ourselves. (*S/R*, 41.)

This is one reason why current theology gives less attention than in the past to "arguments for the existence of God." (*S/R*, 42.)

> ■ *S/R*, 42 seems to be in conflict with the section above. The author of the selected reading says: "I think the assumption that all men have a god of some kind is probably false. . . ." Which viewpoint seems to you to be correct? Why?
>
> ■ How might the concerns of current theology help persons see the heart of the gospel? Divide the class into groups of four to six persons. Each group will study *S/R*, 43. Let members of the group restate in their own words their understanding of each of the emphases of current theology listed in the reading. Which of these emphases express concerns you have felt? Which, if any, do you see as threats to theology as witness to the good news? How do/might these statements help you think new thoughts or free you to think in new ways about your faith? How do/might they help you to be able to give account of your faith?

HOW DID I COME TO KNOW GOD?

Let us assume that we are answering this question as a convinced Christian. I am sure the first thing to say is that I learned about God from my family just as I learned from them how to talk. I can never recall the time when I did not know God. Prayers were said at home. The family worshiped together in church. God was often mentioned in connection with how we should live together. In short, a child breathes the atmosphere of faith as he breathes the very air. But, of course, the child of even the best home has at this stage many "childish" notions about God.

To broaden our answer just a bit: Men learn about their gods from the community into which they are born, just as they learn their language and basic habits of behavior.

But a time comes when the child must take this faith over for himself. Some denominations call this "confirmation." This stage is important. We cannot inherit a faith that we are unwilling to confirm ourselves. We have to sign our own name to it, so to speak.

Until this choice is ratified by me, the God of my parents and community is not yet my God. This time in life between childish and mature faith may be filled with doubts and questions. I must satisfy them enough to make the commitment. It is sometimes a period of intense personal searching.

Young people go through this process in every generation. If the culture they live in is filled with doubts, they will have a more agonizing struggle to decide. But even more important—if the lives of those in my family or church or community who have taught me the words of faith do not conform to the meaning of those words, then the confusion runs very deep. For instance, a child hears his parents say that God is love, and then notices that they do not love their neighbor if the neighbor does not have the same color of skin or political views. What is the child to believe—what he has heard or what he observes?

No generation of adults is able to perfectly harmonize verbal belief and total behavior, so doubt—as well as the beginnings of faith—is passed on to each generation. All of us in the older generation are to blame. Arguments cannot convince if our way of living speaks louder than our words. (*S/R*, 44.)

■ Invite three or four college-age young people to visit your class and discuss with you the difficulties faced by youth in search of a faith of their own.

One member of the class may act as interviewer. He may begin by reading aloud *S/R*, 44. The young people would be ready to respond to questions raised by the interviewer in relation to the reading. (The young people should have copies of the selected reading prior to the class session.) Allow time for other members of the class to raise questions and for the young people to ask questions of the adults.

■ Another possibility would be for three members of your group to be prepared to have a conversation about the reaction of youth to the way adults use traditional religion. Let one person read aloud *S/R,* 44. Then the three persons might discuss these questions: In what respects does the reading present a true and accurate picture? Which statements do you disagree with? Why? Let each person cite specific examples that support or refute the charge that adults use religion for controlling youth and for keeping the social structure stable. Allow time for open discussion by other members of the class.

This lack or harmony between what we profess and the way we live gives rise to a searching for God even within the community of faith.

Job in his distress cried, "Oh, that I knew where I might find him. . . ." (Job 23:3.) Every man echoes this cry at some time or other in his life. It is the search for meaning, for an answer to life's puzzle. It is the search for a god! [Editor's note: This topic was the theme of the first part of Foundation Studies in Christian Faith, *Man's Search for a Meaningful Faith.*]

Jeremiah gives the answer that has been verified through generations of faith, "If you will seek me with all your heart, I will be found by you, says the LORD. . . ." (Jeremiah 29:13-14.) Another translation says, "I will let myself be found by you. . . ." After such a "finding," men of faith usually testify that it was not so much that they found God as that God found them. Faith always recognizes that God's love is the more active side of the searching process. God's letting himself be found is actually his loving strategy in bringing free men fully to himself. (*S/R,* 45.)

■ The idea of God seeking men often appears in poems and hymns. A team or committee might work out an arrangement of "I Sought the Lord," *The Methodist Hymnal,* 96, as a choral reading. Plan the reading so that two or more voices can read responsively, in unison, or as solo voices. Interesting contrasts may be achieved by using light, medium, and heavy voices.

Or the class might simply read the hymn in unison and then discuss this question: How common is the experience described here? How does a person come to such a knowledge or experience?

WHAT OF RELIGIOUS EXPERIENCES?

In this God-search, men are sometimes surprised by experiences that they feel come from God. They may find themselves, for instance, caught up in some mystical moments of certitude and joy. Or in a time of deep doubt or suffering or tragedy, they may sense a comforting power sweeping over them, taking them out of their despair. These experiences may come in moments of prayer and worship, or when contemplating beautiful music or a breathtaking natural scene. (S/R, 46.) Or they may come during a moral struggle to make a wise decision, or perhaps when glimpsing the moral goodness and love of someone else. Such experiences are often marks of the man who is, so to speak, "on his way" spiritually. We should distinguish between "religious" feelings, however, and a commitment to Christ. Many people have the "religious feelings" just described but never get beyond them.

Religious experiences are of many kinds, perhaps as many kinds as there are men. Maybe that is the reason why your religious experience does not convince me, nor mine convince you. Perhaps also that is why we cannot all have the experiences described by saints and mystics. God gives us whatever experiences belong to our temperament and condition in life. The important element in the experience is that it raises the level of life's meaning and gives new heart to the desire for God.

THE SIGNIFICANCE OF REPENTANCE

The earliest New Testament preaching was in this form: Repent and believe in the gospel. The Christian faith has always tied knowing God to repentance and belief. What does this mean?

It means that the prime reason for our failure to know God is our way of living. We organize life around ourselves and evaluate all that happens in terms of the ego. Such an ego-centered being cannot know God without turning outward. That is what conversion means—a turning. And conversion's first step is repentance, regret for the narrow self-centered style of one's life.

After the turning, there is then the believing. At first, this is taken on the word of others—those others whose lives and words have aroused in us the mood of repentance.

But believing is still short of knowing in the New Testament sense. Believing must be tested and deepened by loving. Only if repentance and belief result in a life of loving care for others do we know that the repentance was genuine and the belief profound. (*S/R,* 47.)

LOVING IS KNOWING

Now we come, so to speak, to the "pay-off." Loving leads to knowing God. In the words of John, "We know that we have passed out of death into life, because we love the brethren." (1 John 3:14.) There are good reasons why love and love alone can give us a knowledge of the Christian God.

The first is that the God whom we seek to know is himself love. The second is that one can know love only by loving. Thinking may help us to love; but it cannot know love unless it is joined to the personal will to love without limit. The third reason follows from what was said earlier about the meaning of having a "god." To have a "god," I said, was to worship a given value or being as the highest. To know the God of love, then, would be to worship love as the center of life, to elevate that value to the supreme place. What is that but to love! So if you want to know God, love!

There is another thing that follows from this Christian notion of the way we know God. Knowing God is not merely an individual matter. It grows out of a community of love— which is one good definition of the church at its best. We know God together in a community of unconditional mutual loving-kindness. Does this not also explain why we have our doubts? And why the world does not always believe our proclamations of faith? The way to resolve those doubts is through deeper repentance, more earnest belief, and un-limited love. And if we have visions and ecstasies on the way, we can say so. Under such conditions, the doubters will have reason to suppose that such experiences are mere illusions.

WHAT ABOUT REASON?

Since in earlier years rational arguments have predomi-nated discussions of how we know God, we still must ask about the place of reason in our God-knowing. It has its place. After all, the Word (Logos) that became flesh is not contrary to *logic*. (In the first chapter of John, *word* is logos in Greek.) Logos, the eternal Word, is the principle by which the whole creation hangs together. (Colossians 1:17.) Logic is the set of principles by which arguments hang together. How could they be at odds!

But existing is not mere thinking. Existing as a concrete human being is bigger than thinking. But it does not violate thinking—not if it is Christian living.

How does a mature Christian answer when he is asked why he believes that "reality is love"? He believes this because it is the only principle that makes sense of life as a whole. The concept of a God of creative, sovereign, holy love is the most adequate explanatory principle available to us.

■ Explore and discuss the question of how we may know God. Use "Ways to Knowing God" (Resource Packet, item 5). The Leaders' Guide in the packet contains detailed instructions and questions for discussion.

BUT WHAT OF EVIL?

But does this concept of God as creative, sovereign, holy love account for the evil in the world—especially the suffering of the innocent? That seems to be the main challenge to the Christian claim. How is it to be met?

One way of dealing with this question is to ask another: Suppose a sovereign loving God were making a world to fulfill his purposes. What elements must it contain that also might bring suffering and evil?

1. It would have to be *finite*. That is, it would have to have limits. Only God himself is infinite. This means that its various parts would be limited and dependent upon one another. Death, for instance, would be part of such a world.

2. It would have to be *orderly* and *reliable*. This means that if water, say, were to have the properties it has for quenching our thirst, it will also have the power to drown us if we fall into it. Water cannot suddenly change its properties because a child falls into it. Such a whimsical world would deny finite beings their only basis for learning from experience. It would, for instance, make science, one of man's greatest achievements, impossible.

3. A good world would have to allow *freedom* to men. Puppets could hardly achieve any of the highest levels of human greatness in art, science, or morality. Even religion as a free and loving response to God would be impossible.

But such freedom necessarily includes the possibility that men might turn away from God and even turn on their fellows. God could not suddenly remove their freedom just as they were making mistakes or committing willfully wicked acts. He could do it, yes, but only by canceling the meaning of freedom altogether. A freedom to do only good is no freedom at all.

4. A world that was suitable to carrying out the purposes of infinite love would have to include beings with great *sensitivity*. Otherwise, they could not feel the beauty and goodness of the creation. But if they can feel these things they can also suffer. (*S/R*, 47.)

5. A world designed to bring men to imitate the divine

love would have to be one in which *men are made for one another*. This means that the very conditions in which love can grow are the conditions in which men can be hurt by the selfishness and stupidity of others. I might as a father, for instance, separate my two sons if they quarrel so that the older could not, like Cain, kill or injure his younger brother. But if I kept them apart to prevent injuries, I would also prevent their being true brothers. Leaving them together is the risk a father must run—he prefers brotherly love to safety.

6. A world built for men to grow in must be *capable of improvement*. Another way of putting this is to say that the world must not be finished but on its way to being finished. Nor must man be in a finished state. His growth comes as he faces the challenge of an unfinished world. This is his partnership with the creator God.

If we take these six things together, much of the evil and suffering in the world can be understood as a part of its creation by a God of love. (*S/R,* 48.)

■ How are we to understand evil and suffering in a world created by a loving God? Form at least six small groups. Each group may consider one of the characteristics listed above that allow for both good and evil in the world. If your class is large, more than one group may deal with the same item.

Let each group brainstorm (list without discussion) as many answers as possible to these questions: What good is made possible by this characteristic? What evil is made possible?

When the lists are complete, have someone read aloud *S/R,* 48. Discuss this question in relation to the results of your brainstorming: What actions of ours might divert God's purposes?

A reporter from each group may share briefly the results of their brainstorming and discussion.

THE CHRISTIAN SOLUTION

But the story is not complete. The Christian faith is based upon a story of unspeakable wickedness and suffering— the crucifixion of Jesus Christ. God let Jesus be crucified. He would not deprive men of their freedom even to save his own son. That is part of the meaning.

But our faith teaches us something else about the Crucifixion. It says that God was in Christ suffering for the world. Think this over—God is not *outside* the world watching us suffer. He is *in it,* sharing its growing pangs and its tragedies. Our God is a present God.

How many times have we found that our own difficult moments were lightened by a friend who came along to share them with us. God's presence is like that, only vastly more. He knows our suffering because he shares in it. He comforts and sustains us in it while he suffers it. He is not coolly conducting an experiment with a world which has to suffer; he has taken his place in the center of it.

How does this presence and purpose of the God of holy love make a difference to living? No event, however terrible, is devoid of meaning. (*S/R,* 49.) And if we remember the Resurrection, we can say that no event could ever defeat God's ultimate purposes for his children. In his sovereign creativeness, he cannot be outwitted by his creation. His love will find a way. Perhaps this is the meaning of Paul's saying that "in everything God works for good with those who love him. . . ." (Romans 8:28.)

Such a faith is not a set of mere religious notions to be recited in church. It is a way of life that, in my conviction, has no rival in the world. It offers life—the abundant life— to any who will turn with penitent faith to God and live with expectant love in the world that he has made.

■ The text says that no event, however terrible, is devoid of meaning. Do you agree? Disagree? How would you define meaning? How would you distinguish between the meaning found in one event (the birth of a child) and the meaning found in an entirely different kind of event (the loss of a job)? Have you ever experienced a feeling of the meaninglessness of life? If so, how did you overcome that feeling? How can persons maintain an attitude that makes meaning possible in any situation? Read silently S/R, 49. How do you account for the attitude of the prisoner?

■ To help the group assess their learnings from their study of Chapters 1-5, use side one of the chart "What Have You Learned?" (Resource Packet, item 6). The Leaders' Guide in the packet includes specific directions for its use. Alternate procedures are also included.

■ You might use these questions to evaluate your session: At what point have I grown in my understanding of God? Which of our goals have we reached?

■ Close the session with the benediction "God Be in My Head" (Resource Packet, item 1).

■ Let the leadership team be prepared to give assignments for the next chapter of study and the members of the group be prepared to accept the assignments.

NOTES ON CHAPTER 5

Pages 77-78: John B. Magee, *Religion and Modern Man* (Harper and Row, 1967), page 408. Copyright © 1967 by John B. Magee. Used by permission.

Page 80: Quoted in H. Richard Niebuhr, *Radical Monotheism and Western Culture* (Harper and Row, 1960), page 119. Copyright © 1943, 1952, 1955, 1960 by H. Richard Niebuhr. Used by permission.

PAUL DUCKWORTH

*In discovering Jesus Christ we are
discovering ourselves.*

Read these selections in your Bible:
Ephesians 3:14-21
The dimensions of Christ.

Ephesians 1:3-10
God's plan for his human creation.

2 Corinthians 4:4-6
The light within and the light without.

6
□□

CHRIST AND OURSELVES

"Imagine, a priceless thing like that in clay pots like us."
(2 Corinthians 4:7, Cotton Patch Version.) *

*   *   *

God is the center of our faith. More accurately, we should say that "God-in-Christ" is the center.

We must understand right off that Christianity is not a "Jesus cult." Some people forget that God is known to us as a Trinity, and we cannot divide the Trinity in order to worship the Son to the exclusion of the Father and the Spirit. In the ancient world there were, as Paul said, "Many 'gods' and many 'lords.' " Then he added, ". . . yet for us there is one God, the Father, from whom are all things and for whom

---

■ *As you arrive at your place of meeting, check the assignment chart for specific preparation to be made before the session begins.*
■ *Set goals for your study of this chapter as suggested on page 16.*

we exist, and one Lord, Jesus Christ." (1 Corinthians 8:5-6.)

Christians talk of the Holy Spirit as God, too. But we do not believe in three gods who form some kind of heavenly committee, meeting around a throne in the skies. Of course, we must use symbols when we talk about God. When we forget that we are using symbols, however, and think that we are giving literal accounts, we fall into all sorts of difficulties from which it is impossible to get out. One of the marks of deity is that God cannot be caught within our man-made formulas. That is why, as we have seen, the church wisely called its creeds *symbols*. No language or vocabulary can contain him. The divine Logos (the Word, John 1:1) did not become a creed or a theology; the Logos became a person. And it is only with the greatest care that we keep from distorting that revelation by speaking wrongly of it.

THE TRINITY

We must learn to speak of the Lord God, our Lord Jesus Christ, and our Lord the Spirit in such a way that it brings out the full truth of our relationship to deity. We must avoid sounding like men speaking of round squares, four-sided triangles, or some other contradictory nonsense.

The Trinity symbolizes the richness of Christian experience. No simpler creedal formula will satisfy the demands of that experience.

We know that we owe our lives continually to the God who is the ground of our very existence—that is the *Father*. But it is not enough to speak of God as the transcendent mystery of the world. We know that we have also met this same God at the very center of our humanity—in Jesus Christ, the *Son*. (*S/R*, 50.)

Even that is not enough—though many Christians stop here. We also meet this God in our personal lives, in the life of the church, and in history. Especially do we experience

God in those moments when hope rises in us to surmount the tragedies of existence. Then we know that God is not through with his world, that he is still in it and in us. He is a present God—the *Spirit*—who carries us hopefuly into the mysterious future he has in store for us and for humanity.

The trinity is thus a faithful reflection of Christian experience, not (as some have thought) the result of befuddled theologians making the faith harder for laymen to believe.

JESUS CHRIST——MAN OR GOD?

In A.D. 451 a church council at Chalcedon (pronounced *KAL-see-don*) proclaimed: ". . . We all with one accord teach men to acknowledge one and the same Son, our Lord Jesus Christ, at once complete in Godhead and complete in manhood . . . the distinction of natures being in no way annulled by the union, but rather . . . coming together to form one person. . . ." *

This is called the "Definition of Chalcedon." It is not an explanation. It simply states the faith. It says that we may not deny either Christ's manhood or his divinity.

Questions immediately suggest themselves. By *God,* we mean the Being who is infinite creator, omnipotent (all powerful), omniscient (all-knowing), and omnipresent (present everywhere in his creation). By *man,* we mean a finite creature of limited power and knowledge who is located in time and space.

How can these two sets of characteristics be other than contradictory? To say Jesus is both God and man seems to be saying something like "squares are round" or "white is black."

I suppose the first thing to say is that this is one of God's own mysteries. It is a relationship that is not reducible to the kinds of relationships which characterize things. Squares and circles are indeed incompatible. But deity and manhood are

95

not things in space and time. This will be clearer as we proceed.

What is the nature of man? We learn from Genesis that the very nature of man is to be inspired, that is "breathed into," by God. God formed man of the "dust of the ground" and then awakened him to his existence as man by breathing into him the "breath of life." Thus man shares somehow in God's life simply by being man. His true nature cannot be understood as a mere animal or physical organism.

To be sure, man forgets this divine origin of his life and turns away from the divine Spirit to live by his own personal delusions. That is, he falls into sin.

The point is that man is amphibious. He lives both in the world and in the Spirit. Without that Spirit, he cannot even be a true man.

Jesus is—from one point of view—the Man who opened his whole being to the source of human being, to God. And he thus became the first true Man.

From another point of view, this manhood of Jesus is the work of God's inbreathing Spirit, that makes him the true divine Son, bearing the marks of God's nature. Perfect manhood and true divinity are the point of intersection that God intended in man's creation—and that point is Jesus Christ. (*S/R*, 51.)

There are some areas of human experience that help make this line of thought meaningful—even though it remains a mystery. Take freedom, for instance. When am I most free? I am most free when I am moved by a truth or a goodness that sweeps me up to the highest moments of my existence. In such moments, I go beyond myself. Or rather I am carried beyond myself. Such peak experiences may occur at moments of creation or invention when I am *inspired* by new thoughts. Or they may occur when I am swept up into a courage or self-sacrifice that lies beyond my normal selfish fears.

When men speak of such experiences, they normally use the language of inspiration. Poets and creative scientists talk in the same strange way about things "coming to them" or "inspiring" them. Yet while carried away, so to speak, they are most themselves. Most free. Most human.

If one could live his whole life in such openness, it would be a wonderful life indeed. Jesus Christ lived such a life. And more than that—he inspired others, millions of them, to open themselves to the graciousness of the divine life. (*S/R*, 52.) In so doing, they found that they became more than they dreamed they could be.

These remarks do not explain the mystery of God's way with man. They merely show that the church's talk about Jesus is related to the deepest truths about ourselves. They suggest that in thinking about Jesus we are thinking about ourselves.

When we say of Jesus that he was a man, we are talking about more than Jesus. We are talking about our own future. Are we limited to the kind of human being we presently are? Our faith says NO! The Sonship of Jesus is the down payment, so to speak, on the final state of humanity. In the words of one of the great theologians of the second century, God became man in order that man might become God.

This is why we cannot talk about Jesus without also taking the Holy Spirit into it. The Spirit is the power of God still at work doing in us what he succeeded in doing in Jesus. The Book of Hebrews made this clear. He writes of God's intention to bring "many sons to glory." (Hebrews 2:10.) He says that we "share in a heavenly call." (Hebrews 3:1.) Paul is even clearer: "He destined us in love to be his sons through Jesus Christ." (Ephesians 1:5.)

The point that touches our lives is this: If Jesus was not brought to the fullness of his humanity as the Son, then we cannot hope for that fullness ourselves.

97

■ What qualities or characteristics of Jesus' life have been your inspiration? What about him draws you to him? Compare your ideas and feelings with those described in *S/R, 52*. What factors, do you think, account for any difference that you may find between your ideas and those in the reading?

■ Prior to this session the leadership team might go through the preceding sections and select what they consider to be the two or three key sentences or phrases in each section. These should be written on newsprint or chalkboard for class members to see.

For five minutes, let members of the class suggest questions that are raised in their minds by these sentences or phrases. You may use the words *what, where, how, when, why, who,* to help in stating the questions. Have one person record the questions on chalkboard or newsprint.

Let the whole group consider the questions in these ways: (1) Think together about how the forms of the questions, in a sense, dictate the answers you are able to find and accept. Do this with three or four questions. (2) Can you discover what assumptions lie behind the questions? For example, what are you assuming about the relationship of Jesus and God? About the relationship of Jesus to you? How willing are you to accept these assumptions as answers to the questions, or do you need to engage in further exploration?

BUT WHAT PROOF HAVE WE?

The first thing to say is that this is a faith, not a conclusion of a rational proof. How could we prove what the future holds for man? Perhaps the best we can say is that once we have seen this high possibility for humanity, nothing lower seems quite adequate. That is, no other estimate of the meaning of our humanity arouses in us the same deep response and moves us to our highest achievements.

You could say that the saints are a kind of proof. They are proof in the sense that they are possible only on the basis of such a hope and such a faith. Yet they tower above man's achievements when he is not inspired by this faith.

Another proof is this. Once we have seen what such a view of humanity really means, we cannot live by anything less. We do not *prove* it; we simply cannot help *approving* it. It claims us. It is like seeing what our duty is. Once it is clear, we cannot escape the demand it places upon us. I wonder if this is not what Paul meant when he reversed the usual order of proving and knowing. "If anyone imagines that he knows something, he doesn't yet know what he ought to know . . . But if he loves God, he is known by him." (1 Corinthians 8:2-3.)

This difference between *knowing* and *being known* is fundamental to the Christian's knowledge of God. God as love seeks man out and draws him to his purposes. God takes the initiative. (*S/R*, 53.) And as we find ourselves drawn in this way, we understand who it is who draws and holds us. Knowing God in this sense is more like falling in love than making a scientific discovery.

■ On the basis of the discussion of the possibility of our attaining a greater degree of humanity, study the pictures and Scripture in Bulletin Board Display III (Resource Packet, item 2). Answer the question that accompanies the pictures. Additional questions and suggestions for arranging the display are in the Leaders' Guide in the packet.

ON TALKING ABOUT JESUS CHRIST

If we are to live by our faith in God revealed in Christ, we must take care in talking about Jesus. The divinity of Jesus, for instance, does not mean that he knew everything from the time of his childhood. The church rejected the gospels that told stories about his giving lectures in mathematics on the first day of school. Theologians recognized that a child with infinite knowledge could not be a truly human being.

Similarly the church rejected the gospels that told such stories as the boy Jesus making clay birds which flew off. Such power belongs to the Father, not to the Son. And yet, this is perhaps going too far. Jesus' healings in the Gospels in the New Testament are signs of the present power of the

Kingdom. But even here there is a reserve about the Son's exercise of power that is far short of the omnipotence of the Father.

We need have no reserve in thinking about Jesus as human through and through. His divinity is not the cramping or limiting of his humanity. Nothing is amputated that is needful for a true humanity—except one thing. That one thing is the yielding to selfish wilfullness that marks for the rest of us a turning away from the Father. We close ourselves off from the Father; the Son is open to him. And when we learn that openness from the Son, we too shall learn what true human living can be.

In talking about Jesus' humanity, we must take care not to think of him simply as a religious genius or a very great man. His greatness is his humility toward the Father, his openness. This is why the Christian faith sees in the words and deeds of Jesus the wisdom and graciousness of God. His Crucifixion is both a human faithfulness to the end and a sign of God's suffering presence to men. Something like this must be the meaning of the language about Jesus being a divine sacrifice—that his death is nothing less than God's suffering for men, not merely a martyr suffering for his loyalty to God. (*S/R, 54.*)

By now the difficulty of speaking about the mystery of Christ should be plain. The church has had to correct the faithful when they have gone astray either to the side of the humanity or the divinity of Jesus Christ and thus destroyed the faith. If Jesus' greatness is mere human achievement alone, there is hope only for the geniuses among men. If his life is not human—only an appearance of being human —then God has not come close to our humanity at all. The promise of a sonship like his is then made impossible.

Only the balance of the Chalcedonian definition will do— in Jesus Christ we see both man and God.

■ Jesus is the supreme example of the meeting of the two kinds of existence, humanity and divinity. What is your understanding of the way in which Jesus unites Godhood and manhood? What characteristics or qualities do you attach to Jesus' humanity? to his divinity? Which events or actions attributed to him do you label as human? as divine?

WHY IS LIFE NOT MORE DIVINE?

If this triune faith is the truth about existence, why is our life not more divine? The church's answer is simple: sin. Sin is man's turning from his natural destiny as a child of God toward what he has made of himself. Sin is our lack of openness to God. (S/R, 55.) This closed life makes us selfish, unloving, and uncreative. It also fills us with fears and guilt. Our present so-called "natural life" is really very unnatural. It is like an arm that has begun to turn blue from having a tourniquet on too long. The circulation of blood that makes a healthy limb has been fatally restricted.

Our present state of being is a strangulated life. Jesus came to release us from that life by opening us up to the life of the Father. When we open to him, we find abundant life flowing through us. We become free. As his Spirit becomes more and more our spirit, we are creative again—reflecting the creative nature of God himself.

The Trinity is a perfect symbol for this condition. God made us as beings who breathed in his breath in order to live. We want to live on our own resources—to hold our breath, so to speak. The Son comes and reminds us of our true nature and we breathe freely again. The refreshing oxygen of the Spirit brings life to our whole being. God is the creator; Jesus is the liberator; and the Spirit is the inspirer. (S/R, 56 and 57.)

■ Group discussion: Think of all the possible ways the above definitions of God, Jesus, and Spirit have meaning. How could each person learn to (1) co-operate in God's creative work? (2) avail himself of the liberating power of Jesus? (3) find avenues through which inspiration of the Spirit might come? What assumptions or actions of yours might hinder your participation in this God-man communication? What changes in your thinking, in your mental images of the work of God, Jesus, and Spirit may be necessary for experiences of creativity, liberation, and inspiration to occur?

THE DANGER OF SELF-SALVATION

We live in a country that prides itself on individualism and hard work. It is easy to translate this valuable tradition into a false self-reliance. Our faith tells us that human life cannot come to its fullness without the grace of God. I have used the analogy of blood circulation and breathing. Man is a part of the universe of God and can only come to himself in unity with the source of the creation. When man does not learn to rely on the God of love, he turns to other powers beyond himself to aid him in his uncertainties. He is not as self-reliant as he boasts.

Jesus brings us back to that unity in God. He opens up the way again. (S/R, 58.) The healing blood of the divine love flows again in our lives, cleansing and healing them. The church has talked about the symbolism of blood, but it has sometimes made the wrong use of that symbol. Blood is indeed a vital fluid and a perfect symbol of the new life. (See Deuteronomy 12:23 ". . . the blood is the life. . . .") But it is often tied into an imperfect notion of sacrifice. Some Christians think that Christ suffered because God demanded a blood sacrifice.

■ To clarify the meaning of "blood" where it occurs in connection with Jesus, let someone read aloud Matthew 27:4, Acts 20:28, and 1 Corinthians 10:16 substituting "life" where "blood" appears. John 6:53 says "drink his blood," meaning "take inside oneself his life."

Would such a demand be loving? Would a human father require that before he took his own child back into fellowship with him? We must remember that love is the perfect word for God's nature. The sacrifice of Jesus, I believe, must always be thought of as God's loving self-giving for us—never as a demand by him due to some imagined judgment upon us.

Again, in saying this I am mindful that even in the New Testament one finds expressions of God demanding a blood sacrifice. That is only to say that all of the Bible is not on the high level of God's love. The Bible has a center—that center is the revelation of God in Christ as creative, sovereign, holy love. We must constantly read the Scriptures in that light. Vengefulness in either the Old or New Testaments (see certain parts of the Revelation to John) falls below the full revelation and is not part of God's message to us.

These remarks are not an attempt to use human standards to judge the Bible. They are an effort to use the center of the Bible (God-in-Christ) to interpret the Bible as a whole. It is a biblical interpretation through and through. There is no other place that I know of but in the Bible that such a revelation of holy love appears in this world. I am afraid that a certain kind of biblical literalism still lingers in many of us. We should rid ourselves of this barrier to the faith once and for all. The church has never been literalist in this sense, even if occasionally its great figures have not been aware of the degree to which they contributed to such a notion. (*S/R,* 59.)

THEOLOGY AND THE BIBLE

These remarks suggest how important theology is for our use of the Bible itself. The Bible is indeed the standard for all our theology, but it is not itself a system of theology. It is the record of events and teachings, the life and faith of the first saints of God. It is the primary source for our knowledge of Jesus—and through him of our knowledge of God.

But the Bible cannot be used without thought. And it cannot be thought about rightly without the inspiration of the Spirit. The Spirit is, as I have said, the power of new speech, a new communication. But biblical literalism has historically fostered a spirit of division—often bitter division. Even today as the Holy Spirit moves among the churches to bring them closer together, it is the literalists who bitterly denounce all these attempts at a new understanding. I do not say they are insincere. I say that they are still under the curse of Babel—spreading misunderstanding and uncharitableness even within the household of faith.

These words need a postscript. In one sense, the literalists have fought a good fight to keep elements in our faith that seemed likely to be lost. They have tried to keep elements in our faith that humanistic liberalism was too willing to let go. I honor them for that.

But the liberal movement was itself too literal minded. Liberalism has been so influenced by scientific thought that it lost the understanding of the great symbols of Christianity. These symbols cannot be translated into humanistic or scientific language. Understanding the Trinity, for instance, requires a kind of imagination and poetic understanding that is as far from the liberal mind as it is from the biblical literalist. With our modern understanding of language, these misunderstandings should soon come to an end among sincere men of both persuasions.

CONCLUSION

Throughout this chapter I have tried to point out that as theology deals with the nature of Christ, the Trinity, and human nature it is not simply engaging in a game of obscure notions. It is trying to clarify the living issues at stake in the task of understanding our faith.

What is at stake? The nature of our humanity and our future is at stake. What are the resources available to man in his effort and us in our effort to be really human? Where is freedom to move creatively into the open future? Our faith says that it is in God's action through Christ. It is in the gift of the Spirit to us as an ever-present breath of life.

■ Evaluate this session. Which of your goals were achieved? If some were not, what hindered your achievement of them? What steps need to be taken to avoid the same mistakes?

■ Pray together the benediction "God Be in My Head" (Resource Packet, item 1).

■ Let the leadership team be prepared to give assignments for the next chapter of study and the members of the group be prepared to accept the assignments.

■ At this point it is time to place your order for the fifth unit of study, *Dimensions of Decision:* Christian Ethics as Witness to the Good News.

NOTES ON CHAPTER 6

Page 93: *The Cotton Patch Version of Paul's Epistles* by Clarence Jordan (Association Press, 1968), page 79. Used by permission.

Page 95: Quoted in *Documents of the Christian Church,* edited by Henry Bettenson (Oxford University Press, 1963), page 73. Copyright 1963 by Oxford University Press.

Read these selections in your Bible:
Matthew 10:5-8
The kingdom of heaven is at hand.

Matthew 13:31-33, 47-50
A mustard seed and a fish net.

Matthew 20:20-23
Lord, we are able!

Matthew 22:1-10
The Kingdom is like a marriage feast open to all.

Matthew 25:1-13, 31-46
The Kingdom includes judgment.

7
□□□□□□□□□□□□□□□□□□□□□□□□□□□□□□□□□□□□□□□

THE FUTURE OF MAN

"I am increasingly persuaded that the Lord God is not viewing all this 'from the beginning' to see where his creation might wind up . . . or run down; nor is he at the end of time with some predetermined blueprint before him, watching the mockery of freedom and the meaninglessness of individual decision.

"But I believe that God is always halfway through eternity, that at this moment he is at work to complete creation . . . moving from the center to every part of an expanding universe. I am convinced that God is not seeking a way out but longs for those who will share his infinite patience with the world to penetrate it, participate in it and redeem it. He

■ *As you arrive at your place of meeting, check the assignment chart for specific preparation to be made before the session begins.*
■ *Set goals for your study of this chapter as suggested on page 16.*

is not so much 'heavenly father' as 'companion on the way.'
So be it." *

           *   *   *

In the preceding chapter I have tried to show that the
Christian faith is about and for man. Christ was the man for
others—the model of love. And Christ is God's love for all
men. He is also the measure of man's future and the hope of
his coming to human fullness. The Nicene Creed says that
God became man "for us and for our salvation."

CONSIDER HISTORY

To believe in progress is to have faith in continuous development, each level being more beneficial than and superior
to previous levels of attainment.

Most of us have believed in progress from our childhood
up. This belief grew in a scientific climate and was nourished
by the optimism of European and American life from the
seventeenth century until early in the twentieth century.
Some thought that each generation moved a little closer to
perfection than the previous one.

The twentieth century has begun to have doubts about
progress. For instance, we have seen Germany—Europe's
most literate and scientific nation—turn back to pagan bar-
barism and use scientific methods to kill millions of innocent
people. We have also seen the great blessings of science turn
into curses in our own hands. (S/R, 60.) We have witnessed
the coming of the monster of nuclear weapons and a population explosion that threatens to crowd civilized life off the
planet.

These problems have caused us to wonder whether men
were automatically becoming more perfect. If we had believed the New Testament, we never would have been so
simple-minded as to have accepted the notion of the natural

107

goodness of man or its logical by-product, the notion of automatic progress.

The notion of automatic progress is like an escalator that moves upward. Every later period is supposed to be better than its predecessor. Only a few people, ourselves among them, have ever believed this.

In the Far East, the view of history is like a merry-go-round. History moves in circles. This cyclical (from the word *cycle,* a circle) view of history suggests that history can have no real meaning or direction. Everything repeats itself. This view even appears in our Bible. The writer of Ecclesiastes said, "There is nothing new under the sun." (1:9.)

What is the Christian view of history? There is unfortunately no easy way to diagram it like a line or a spiral or a circle. According to the Bible, history is the story of man's salvation. It includes a notion of progress, but it is progress in a special sense. The progress is God's transformation of history into the kingdom of God. It is also God's transformation of man into the "fullness of Christ." (Ephesians 4:13.)

If we tried to make a diagram of this Christian notion, we might think of a horizontal line with another series of lines running vertical to it. The horizontal line is the line of history; the vertical lines are God's continuous disruption and salvation of that history.

The kingdom of God is not an earthly utopia. It is not a model society based, say, on democracy or some other political view. Nor is the future of some particular type of man drawn from one culture or another. Both the kingdom of God and the "fullness of Christ" ideas lie *beyond* history.

And yet this Kingdom represents all the good that God intends to achieve through human history.

Jesus said that the Kingdom is *already here.* (See Luke 10:8-9; 11:20; 17:20-21.) This means that the sovereign power is even now overcoming all the kingdoms of the world —all the powers that restrict and confine man. Jesus illustrated this in healing a child. The healing is a mark of the liberating power that is already present.

But the Kingdom is also *not yet here.* (See the Bible readings at the beginning of this chapter.) Nor is it ever fully here—as long as history lasts. For no period of history, no country, no social system, and no culture can contain this fullness that belongs only to God. That is why we must be careful when we talk about "bringing in" the Kingdom. When we act with faith under God's sovereign power, we do indeed bring in the Kingdom in a very literal sense. But we must beware of thinking that, say, the American Way of Life, if perfected a bit here and there, would be the Kingdom.

Is this understanding of the past just another strange speculation of ivory tower theologians? Or is it the fevered imagination of the writers of those hard to interpret passages in the New Testament? If it is neither, it suggests a way of life different from any other and emerges from the central meaning of our faith.

In the first place, it removes from us all sorts of foolish beliefs—such as the innate goodness of man or the automatic, escalator view of progress. This might seem to take away the hope of improving our lives. Not at all! Actually it greatly increases such prospects, because it places our hope where it belongs—in God and his continual action for us through love.

In the second place, it keeps us from the disillusionment and despair that come when the facts of human life undermine our confidence in man and progress. The Christian can never despair of man or of the world—because we are in God's hands.

In the third place, when we put our personal lives, our country, and the world in God's hands, things begin to happen that lead to real advances. These advances are never to be equated with the final purpose he has for us, however.

He always has more. We must never put limits on his work on man's behalf. When we realize this, the future is really open for us. What is not possible for man is possible for God.

Does this result in sitting down and waiting? A good question. Some Christians have thought this in the past. They were mistaken. The creator God asks us to trust him as we work and create under his loving guidance. He brings us into partnership in our own self-making and in the making of human history. Sitting quietly by and tolerating evils in the world or in ourselves is a betrayal of his love. (S/R, 61.)

This view of God's kingdom is an invitation to dynamic action, not to sitting idly by. No human arguments may be used to make the Christian satisfied with life as it is. Under this faith, men are led to the most resolute action against the ills that beset us. They are resolute, because men of faith do not trust only in themselves but in the God who is the sovereign power of history. (S/R, 62.)

■ Some people accept the idea of the natural goodness of men. Read S/R, 60. How does this deny the belief in the innate goodness of man? Cite examples from the present that would deny the idea.

■ Contrast the biblical concept of the kingdom of God with the secular notion of perfection of society. Work in groups of four to six persons. Each group should study at least two of these passages: Matthew 13:24-30, 31-33, 44, 45-46, 47-50; 22:1-10; 25:1-13. What is your view of what the passage is moving toward? Compare your view with the notion of progress as related to the Christian view of history discussed above. Do you lean toward the view of the perfection of society, or the biblical concept of the kingdom of God? Why?

■ The text lists three reasons why the Christian view of history is different from other views. See also S/R, 62. Discuss these questions in relation to the three reasons: (1) Why does giving up a belief in the innate goodness of man cause us to place our hopes in God? Does it always? Why? Why not? (2) What facts of human life might undermine our confidence in man? (3) What aspects of the world, our country, our personal lives can we put into God's hands? In what ways can we do this?

HOW ABOUT A SCIENTIFIC VIEW OF HISTORY?

One popular notion among social scientists is that history, like the motion of the stars, is bound to natural law. We can predict eclipses; why not predict everything that happens in society? This notion derives its strength from the successes of science in the study of nature.

If it is true, then we must take a very gloomy view of human affairs. Freedom is an illusion. None of our acts can make any difference. The future is bound completely to the past.

Applied to the individual—to you, for instance—it means that all that you are or ever will be is contained in the chemical reactions that led to your birth. As the biologists say, you *are* your *genes,* the tiny molecules that pass on heredity from one generation to another. Once born, you are nothing but a bag of chemicals and with nature to produce every act of your existence. (S/R, 63.)

Applied to society, this view means that every event in society is understandable as the result of prior history.

By contrast, the Christian faith believes in the open future for individuals and for societies. Life is an episode of continuous creativity in interaction with the creator God who entered history in Christ and who is present among us as the Spirit. Life is not a result of the past alone. It is the result of creative decision in every moment, in a setting that includes our past. Such is the meaning of the diagram of history with the vertical lines intruding upon the horizontal line.

And what does that view mean to us? It means that we can never excuse ourselves by saying, "I can't help what I am." We can never truly say, "My future is determined by my past." That lock step has been broken by grace, by God's liberating action. (S/R, 64 and 65.)

This should remind us of some things said earlier. We cannot prove this creative freedom by proofs that appeal to facts. For the facts are the things that seem to determine us in a scientific way. Our proof—if we are to have one—lies in laying hold on this freedom through faith and demonstrating by the way we live the creative power of life under God.

In society it would prove itself by attempting the so-called impossible task of ridding the world of age-old evils like war and human injustice. Christians are not mere idealists. They do not believe that ideals have a way of automatically becoming facts. They live by faith in the sovereign power of God. What is impossible to men, they say, is possible to God.

Through prayer and repentance, the greatest changes can take place in individuals. Lifelong habits can be changed and deep-seated prejudices can be uprooted. Through the faith of the creative action of the community of faith, history can be changed. (S/R, 66.)

Notice how Jesus leads the way. Think how different history is because of him. Just one man—but God was in him working out his purposes for mankind.

■ Select two persons to read S/R, 64 and 65. Follow the readings carefully as they read. Here are two contrasting approaches to freedom. What do they mean to you? Which view is closer your view? How did you arrive at the view you hold? What reasons might be cited to support the view that man's freedom is only an illusion? What evidence denies this view? When people say, "I can't help what I am," do they expect praise or blame? What attitudes toward oneself and life do you think underlie this statement?

■ Assuming that history needs to be changed where you are, how might you use the pattern in S/R, 66 as a source for a plan of action? Study the reading carefully. A member of the leadership team might guide the reading, stopping the group at points along the way to analyze the actions being described. Where would you have acted differently?

Perhaps the group would like to choose a hypothetical problem and, using the reading as a guideline, set up steps they might go through to bring about change. Then give serious consideration to where you as a group might work for change. How might you go about it?

THE LIFE EVERLASTING

Everlasting life is by far the most commonly accepted Christian idea of eschatology, the end or goal of life. (Theologians use the word *eschatology* to talk about these "last things.") Unfortunately, we have emphasized everlasting life almost to the exclusion of the notion of the kingdom of God. Jesus spoke much more often about the Kingdom than about everlasting life.

Perhaps this is due to the fact that the earliest Christians saw little hope of a real transformation of society. On the other hand, they were flooded with light as they thought about the Resurrection. They quite naturally narrowed the Christian hope down to individual immortality. (*S/R,* 67.)

Do not misunderstand me. Life everlasting is an important part of the Christian hope. No faith could call itself Christian that did not take this belief seriously. It is a symbol of the absolutely open future that lies before us as individuals.

But even this hope has been distorted in our thinking. Let us see how. First, consider the notion of heaven and hell.

The Christian faith in the open future for man became very early literalized into an option between two places, heaven and hell. Those who were "saved" went to heaven and those not saved were damned to an eternal hell. The kernel of truth in these conceptions do not save them from being gross distortions of the New Testament faith in God's purposes for man.

In what ways are they distortions? First of all, salvation is not a ticket to a place. It is a power to become a truly human person in the likeness of Christ. A person whose life has been transformed by this power passes triumphantly over the death line, assured that God has much more in store. If salvation did not change us into new persons fit for fellowship with God and with one another, any place would become the same kind of place the earth presently is. Golden streets and gem-studded furniture would not make that much difference.

The imagery of heaven is to be understood symbolically, not literally. The images are a poetic way of saying that God's provision for man is beyond the limits of our poor earthbound imagination.

A short time before the great Jewish philosopher Martin Buber died in 1965, he was interviewed on British television. He was asked about what lies on the other side of death. He replied: "I think death is the end of everything that we are able to imagine. Therefore, this means that we cannot, and we should not, imagine life after death merely as a going on in time. Time is just something that we know in this life here, just as we know space; and just as space, so time is being omitted from eternity. I don't even imagine a going on in time, but I am certain of entering eternity. And though I cannot imagine it, I know I shall enter it, and *this means that one can be more certain of God's existence than of his own existence.*" *

Buber, I think, is right—and, in this, very Christian. We cannot imagine in detail what this "going on" means. We must learn to trust God with it.

It will be a life of love. It will be a fellowship of some unimaginable sort with God and with one another. But we would be wise to abstain from too detailed an account of these things. Faith does not require it. The Christian must be satisfied with the certainty that God has prepared a future for and with him.

■ Read silently *S/R, 67*. Discuss: What is the relationship of the kingdom of God and immortality according to this reading? Do you find any clues to why Jesus spoke more often about the Kingdom than about eternal life? How does the reading support the definition of salvation in the text? What is the "kernel of truth" in the early interpretation of everlasting life as heaven for the "saved" and hell for the "damned"? Does questioning the existence of pearly gates and streets of gold cause you to feel that the reality of everlasting life is being questioned? If so, why do you think it so important to know these physical details? How do you respond to Buber's concept of life after death?

Christians have distorted the message more in talking of hell than of heaven. Before saying more, we should remember that we are talking about the eternal purposes of a God of unlimited love. We are talking about the purposes of the God who did not spare his own Son to reveal his nature to humanity.

The Gospels plainly teach that some awful punishment awaits unrepentant sinners. (*S/R*, 68.) The figures that attempt to describe the terror of that punishment are fire and worms. *Gehenna* and *hades* are the words used in the New Testament.

Very early in the history of the church the idea arose that the soul would be purified by this punishment and that eventually all souls would be saved. Space in this book does not allow a full development of the belief in the long history of the church that salvation would come to all sinners. This belief in *universalism* (that all would someday be saved) arose out of the conviction that a God who is love would not allow punishment to go on everlastingly but would use the punishment as a means of redemption. Though the justice of God, they said, would require some punishment for the unrepentant sinner, the love of God suggests that the punishment have as its goal not vengeance but penitence.

Among some Christians, hell has been talked about in such a way that the very nature of God has been transformed into a monstrous demon who delights in the fiendish tortures of those who did not please him. Worse than that, this doctrine has even been applied to those who through no fault of their own never heard of Christ. Some churches have even talked about newborn babes going to hell if they were not baptized before their deaths.

Could anyone imagine anything more unjust—not to say unloving!

What are we to make of this doctrine? Let us begin by pointing out a basic truth. Life apart from God and his purposes is like an arm cut off from the blood supply of the body—it is poisoned by its own chemicals and finally dies. Sin—the turning away from God into one's own self—is like that, and its consequences are terrible. We need no lessons on that. Everyday experience shows the consequences of a life turned away from goodness into vice and evil.

Hell is symbolic of the inevitable consequence of evil. But our understanding of it must be seen against the background of God's grace. Hell should not be thought of as an instrument of vengeance. In his love, God intends that every life shall eventually come to him and to its own fullness. Unlike human love, God is not angry when spurned. He does not become impatient. (See First Corinthians 13.) I am convinced that he cannot be outwitted. He has time and he made men for himself. Thus he can wait for the moment in which each life becomes sick of its own self-made hell and turns to the light.

We can trust the fate of "pagans" to a father like the one Jesus told us about in the parable of the prodigal son. (Luke 15:11-32.) The "waiting father" would have been a better name for that parable, for it is about God's patience and forgiveness. He waits for men to come to themselves and turn toward him. At that moment, they begin to live again—no matter when it may occur.

■ Read again the foregoing discussion of hell. Then have one person read aloud *S/R,* 68.

What kind of response do you have to the reading? Do you believe this as a possibility for your own end? Why? Why not? What evidence does Jonathan Edwards have for making such statements? What evidence do you see in the life and attitudes of Jesus that God is like this? Edwards was preaching to convert people. Do his words have that effect on you today? What effect do they have? Contrast the interpretation in the text with that in the reading.

HOW DO WE KNOW?

What reasons have we to suppose that such a loving destiny awaits human beings?

The only unshakable foundation for our confidence in eternal life is in the nature of God as Jesus revealed it. It is the God who gave himself to us in love through Christ that can be trusted with our lives now and forever. If he is indeed creative, sovereign, holy love, we need not fear. (S/R, 69.)

What "intimations of immortality" do we have? Harry Emerson Fosdick once used a parable to make this point. Imagine, he said, that twins being formed in the body of the mother can talk to each other. One of the twins says that he thinks their present life is the one and only existence. What we call birth, this twin imagines to be death.

The other twin is not so sure. He does not know, but he has some questions. What are these eyes for if not to see, he asks? What are these feet for, if not to walk, or these hands if not to grasp things with? And how about these lungs? Are they not to breathe air? Of course, a being in such an environment would not be able to imagine the life to come. He could only point to the fact that his present existence seems to point to something more in store. Only such a future would make sense of his own nature.

Just so, the wise human being would be able to point to his own growth in the spirit as a kind of preparation for something far beyond the present existence. A great teacher of mine who was near the end of his career said, wistfully, "One only learns to live just as life draws to a close." The ripe wisdom of age—not just age in years—suggests a preparation of some use to which this wisdom will be put. It is as though the spiritual organs have begun to mature, just as the limbs

117

of an embryo toward the end of its term, and are a preparation for some birth into a greater life.

What spiritual organs do I refer to? I mean the power to
love. The growth of true moral responsibility of character.
I mean the growing communion of prayer and the pervasive
sense of the presence of God in the whole of life. (S/R, 70.)

And there are other things. Death is something that happens to the body not the spirit. There is no reason why it
should die. For that matter neither is the personality the
body. Have we not all seen the body of some fine person
wither away while the person himself shines brighter than
ever in suffering and in the face of death? The whole spiritual
life is in this sense a preparation for a death that is really a
rebirth into a new dimension.

■ Read again the preceding section. Discussion in the group: How
is spiritual growth as "a kind of preparation for something beyond"
different from a way of earning entrance into eternal life? What
ways of thinking may lead one to thinking of spiritual growth as
something that ends with death? What evidences and assumptions
lead you to one of these views?

■ Read silently S/R, 70. Then let persons share, in turn, their
responses to these questions: How did you feel as you read the
excerpt? Why do you suppose you felt as you did? How is your
understanding of meditation similar to/different from that in the
reading? What difference would it make in your life if you accepted
and put into practice Boyd's definition of meditation—". . . a re-
flective openness to the situations we confront daily . . ."?

A FINAL WORD

The great historian Herbert Butterfield concluded his book
Christianity and History with this advice. "There are times
when we can never meet the future with sufficient elasticity
of mind, especially if we are locked in the contemporary
systems of thought. We can do worse than remember a
principle which both gives us a firm Rock and leaves us with
the maximum elasticity for our minds: the principle: *Hold*

to Christ, and for the rest be totally uncommitted [italics mine]." *

If we remember that Christ here means "God-in-Christ," not just Jesus the man, we can live expectantly looking into that open future that God has for us whether in this life or in the next. *(S/R, 70.)*

■ Evaluate this session: Did you see evidence that persons (you) acquired information, new viewpoints, or changed attitudes? What progress was made toward goals set at the beginning of the session?
■ Pray together "God Be in My Head" (Resource Packet, item 1).
■ Let the leadership team be prepared to give assignments for the next chapter of study and the members of the group be prepared to accept the assignments.

NOTES ON CHAPTER 7

Pages 106-7: From a speech given by Robert Albertson at the University of Puget Sound in Tacoma, Washington, 1966.

Page 114: Quoted in *The Listener* (British Broadcasting Corporation), January 18, 1962, page 127. Copyright by Martin Buber. Used by permission.

Pages 118-19: Herbert Butterfield, *Christianity and History* (Charles Scribner's Sons, 1950), page 146. Copyright 1949, 1950 by Charles Scribner's Sons. Used by permission.

TETE DE FEMME, BY PABLO PICASSO, COURTESY OF THE ART INSTITUTE OF CHICAGO

Are you the person God intended you to be?

Read these selections in your Bible:
2 Corinthians 4:3-7
The eternal light in an earthen vessel.

2 Corinthians 3:17-18
Changed into the likeness of the Lord.

Galatians 2:20
We are lived by Christ from within.

Ephesians 4:13
Mature manhood is the measure of Christ.

8

□□

A THEOLOGY OF OUR PERSISTENT PERSONAL CONCERNS

"The origin of all conflict between me and my fellow men is that I do not say what I mean, and that I do not do what I say. For this confuses and poisons, again and again and in increasing measure, the situation between myself and the other man, and I, in my internal disintegration, am no longer able to master it but, contrary to all my illusions, have become its slave. By our contradiction, our lie, we foster conflict-situations and give them power over us until they enslave us. From here, there is no way out but by the crucial realization: Everything depends on myself, and the crucial decision: I will straighten myself out.

■ *As you arrive at your place of meeting, check the assignment chart for specific preparation to be made before the session begins.*
■ *Set goals for your study of this chapter as suggested on page 16.*

"But in order that a man may be capable of this great feat, he must first find his way from the casual, accessory elements of his existence to his own self; he must find his own self, not the trivial ego of the egotistic individual, but the deeper self of the person living in a relationship to the world. And that is also contrary to everything we are accustomed to." *

*   *   *

■ Recall a situation from your childhood or teen years when you were in the position of "I do not say what I mean, . . . I do not do what I say." How did you get into the situation? How closely does the above quotation describe the situation in which you found yourself? Did you straighten the situation out yourself? If so, how were you able to do so?

At this point we are going to attack the problems of theology from a new angle. In Chapter 1 we asked the question, What is theology? Our answer: Theology is faith in search of understanding. Through theology we try to clarify with our minds what our inherited faith really means. We discovered that in this way theology is also one of the many ways to witness to the gospel.

In Chapters 2-4 the path of our search was through history. We traced the variations of theological thought from New Testament times up through the Protestant Reformation. This historical theme will be brought up to date in Chapter 11 when we take a broad look at the world since the seventeenth century. This is the period that historians call the modern world.

Chapters 5-7 were a brief outline of some of the main themes in theology—God, Christ, and Man.

In Chapters 8-10 we are going to look at theology as a way of dealing with primary personal and social concerns. I want to show that theology clarifies and supports them in a special and fundamental way. This approach challenges any theology that is isolated from the affairs of real living. I hope that this idea is already clear from previous discussions. But it should become clearer with this more direct approach.

Let us turn to the positive personal concerns that faith illuminates.

WHO AM I?

Here is a central question. It is implicit in the discussion in the previous chapter. Only a human being can ask this question. A dog or a cat or a tree cannot ask it. These animals and plants are just what they are. But human beings are continually making choices. These choices make us what we are. But as the image of ourselves grows out of the accumulated choices of our lives we may not like what we see. (*S/R*, 71.)

We may ask whether our choices have been right. Would it have been better to move in another direction? Have I missed the self that God intends for me? Is there some new directive for my life? The man who cannot find a satisfactory answer to these questions cannot become a complete man. (*S/R*, 72.)

Erik H. Erikson, in his celebrated book, *Young Man Luther* (W. W. Norton and Company, 1958), tells the story of Luther's quest for personal identity. Luther's search has a message for each of us. Luther's father wanted him to be a lawyer, to settle down, and to have children. Young Luther rejected this view of himself. His resistance to his father's desire to have him marry and become a lawyer had made him very anxious. He had become more and more unable to live well. During a thunderstorm when he thought he might be struck by lightning, he suddenly renounced this parental prison and took the only way open to him—the life of a monk. But he found no immediate answer to his personal quest in the monastic life.

Once during these early years he fell to the floor of the choir of the monastery at Erfurt roaring with the voice of a bull: "It isn't me! It isn't me!" Erik Erikson believes that this exclamation was Luther's rejection of the monk's life as an answer to the question, Who am I? But he had at the time nowhere else to go, no other calling to which to turn. He remained in the monastery and continued his search. Part of the problem lay in the fact that the church of his age had no answer for Luther. He had to reform the church to find his answer. (*S/R*, 73.)

There is a parallel to this in our own day. Can we honestly say to any young man that if he turns to the church and faithfully follows its advice he will find himself? Many honest Christian leaders believe that the institutional church of our own day is as empty of answers for modern youth as was the church of Luther's day. A young man once said to me, "I am less myself in the church than anywhere else." What did he mean?

I suspect that he meant this: The conventional image of what it means to be a Christian seems to many young adults to be a prison of falseness and hypocrisy. No honest young person will want to commit himself to such an institution. (See again *S/R*, 9.)

Luther found it necessary to reform the Christianity of his day before he could find his identity as a Christian man. He had to cut through all the traditions and forge a new image of the Christian life. This situation requires great personal suffering. Growing up is hard enough even if the society is healthy. But if the society in which he lives offers no real options for being fully human, then he must bear the heavy burdens of a new search for truth along with the burdens of his personal search for identity. (*S/R*, 74.) Luther was a very great man and had the ability to succeed in the face of heavy odds.

One of the urgent reasons for undertaking seriously the work of rethinking our faith is to establish a kind of Christian understanding that can offer a live option to human beings—young and old—in our own time.

124

Personal identity is always closely related to the question of whom or what one must obey. Could it be one's father, the state, the pope, or God? But which God? In turning to the church, young Luther thought he had found his answer.

As he persisted in his religious life, he undertook studies in the Bible. It was in the Bible that he began first to discover some possible answers to his problems. As he began, quietly at first, to defend these new insights, he came into conflict with his religious superiors. In time, as we all know, he led the great reformation. We think of this as a religious and social movement. But for Luther, according to Erikson, it was merely the outward side of his personal search for identity. He found it in obedience to the Christ who came to him through faith as he pondered the Scriptures. He became Luther the reformer.

■ Read silently S/R, 72. Engage in some self-examination. Ask yourself: How true of me is this poem? How does this condition affect my style of life? How does this truth about me affect my theological thinking?

■ Discuss: What is your reaction to the young man's words quoted on page 124 about himself and the church? Do you agree with the interpretation of it in the text? Why? Why not?

Listen as one person reads aloud S/R, 9. How did you feel as you read or heard this being read for the first time? Have you ever felt about the church as the young man felt? To whom did you express it? In what sense do his words—*false gentility, empty sentiment, emotional impoverishment, intellectual mediocrity, spiritual tepidity*—accurately describe the church as you know it? In what sense do you consider them harsh or inaccurate? Are we as members of the church guilty of not really listening to criticism because the truth may hurt? How do we justify this? What reinterpretation of the faith is called for in this situation?

■ Evaluate the church's effort and ability to help persons find their identity. Ask a committee to evaluate sermons preached in church for several Sundays, as well as sermons on radio, on the basis of what they say persons ought to be. They might also listen to what gospel songs say. The committee would need to be chosen several weeks in advance of the session so that they are ready to report their observations and conclusions in this session.

WHAT HAS GOD TO DO WITH MY IDENTITY?

Many men seem to be happy with their situation in life today. But there are fewer of these satisfied people today for reasons I have mentioned. The great meanings by which human beings live now are hotly debated. Many men find it impossible to accept the official formulations of these meanings—the official religious meanings that the institutional church teaches. Millions of people in formerly Christian countries have chosen fascism or communism in preference to the meaning of life the church teaches. In America, many have accepted a secular humanism as a solution.

A central idea in the meaning of personal identity is: You are the thing you worship. The being, or value, or idea that you hold central in life defines who you are. Personal identity for a Christian would come at the moment that he found the God of sovereign, creative, holy love as the highest value of his life. Once a man finds his "god," he finds himself. But a false god means a false and unsatisfying identity.

A young man once came to me with the story of his conversion to communism. Before he became a communist, he said, he had had a seemingly incurable stutter in his speech. After he adopted communism, he could speak clearly for the first time in his life. But the stuttering returned when communism failed to answer his needs. When he came to me, he was in search of a new identity. He wanted to know whether the Christian faith could supply him that identity.

■ As you study this chapter contemplate these words, "You are the thing you worship." Study the paragraph in which the statement appears. Try to put your thoughts about it in a two-line verse. You might begin, "The God that I worship . . . ."

EACH FAITH IS A WAY OF LIFE

A faith is a way of life. Each of the great religions teaches men to travel a certain road in their pilgrimage through human existence. When a person chooses a way of life, this identity locates him in the world and in the human community. It suggests a scale of values and gives priority to some values over others. It indicates, too, a personal style of life, including its underlying emotional tone. (*S/R,* 75.)

Against this background of the search for meaning and finding faith as a way of life, let us restate the meaning of faith. We have been describing what I call an "incarnational faith." I mean by that phrase to suggest that we take seriously God's full entrance into human existence through Jesus Christ. I mean also to suggest that God's continued incarnating presence (the Holy Spirit) is in the church and in each one of us. I emphasize the word *incarnating* because I believe that it is God's intention to be fully present to us as grown sons in the likeness of Jesus.

What difference does it make if this faith becomes *my* faith? Immediately we discover a set of priorities in our values. If the God of love is fulfilling himself through us, we will make choices that will allow the fullest personal life possible for every individual whom we influence. The welfare of persons will be the ultimate test of all our actions.

What difference would this choice of a personal faith make in the emotional tone of our life? An immense one, I think. The Christian views this world not as "nature" but as "creation." Wherever God is creating, he is providentially present and acting. He is moving the world toward the goal of the kingdom of God. The emotional tone of such a life will be joy. Not pleasure, but joy—joy that is born of struggle and voluntary suffering on behalf of others. It is an experience of the power of the Resurrection that always follows upon taking up the cross with Jesus.

This choice means that each of us can find his calling—his vocation—under God. He can know why he is here and why he acts as he does. The ultimate test of every decision will be the welfare of persons. This is the Christian way to personal identity. It is not a general or abstract kind of identity, because our God calls each of us by our own name. He gives to each of us a task in his world suited to our powers and our life situation. We must discover what task he gives us. It may not be prominent but it will be directed toward human welfare. As the blind poet, John Milton, wrote, "They also serve who only stand and wait."

Since God speaks to each of us through his Holy Spirit, we can be sure that if we desire to take our place in the world under his guidance, he will let us know what that place is. He will give us the gift of true freedom by which we may progressively become a true man, the new man forecast for us in Jesus.

MATURITY

For a long time, psychologists spent all their energies describing the behavior of human beings. Lately they have recognized that the one thing that characterizes a mature human being as distinct from all other beings is growth. More than that, man is a being whose choices determine his growth. A dog grows from a puppy into a full-grown dog, but he does not make any decisions along the way. He simply grows older.

Human beings unconsciously aim at something more than they are. Maturity is a word for that aim. Psychologists have undertaken to describe what a mature person would be like. In the list of characteristics that follow, notice how many of them fit into the Christian view of persons.

1. Having the ability to deal constructively with reality.
2. Having the capacity to adapt to change.
3. Having a relative freedom from symptoms that are produced by tensions and anxieties.
4. Having the capacity to find more satisfaction in giving than receiving.

5. Having the capacity to relate to other people in a consistent manner with mutual satisfaction and helpfulness.

6. Having the capacity to sublimate, to direct one's instinctive hostile energy into creative and constructive outlets.

7. Having the capacity to love.* (S/R, 76.)

■ Look at the above characteristics of maturity. In the entire group talk about what each one means.

Now, let each person write his answer to this question: What changes do I need to make to achieve a greater degree of maturity in each of these? Take it a step further by writing your intention to make some of these changes. Complete this statement in relation to those you are willing to work on. I will ——————————— ———————————. Keep this card where you can refer to it periodically. Pencils and 3 by 5 inch cards should be provided.

■ Invite an expert in the field of counseling to visit your class to be interviewed on the subject of maturity. A committee or team should have some questions ready to ask of the visitor. Other questions may be raised by members of the group.

Your pastor may be able to help you contact such a person, or appropriate social agencies in your area may refer you to available persons.

MATURITY AND A MATURE FAITH

Achieving such maturity requires a mature faith. A faith, like a person, can be childish and immature. What are some of the characteristics of a mature faith? I will attempt a short list that I am sure you will be able to extend for yourself.

1. A mature faith is comprehensive. It extends to all areas of life, personal and social. Immature faith is always limited to one sphere—a kind of "Sunday faith." A faith in the kingdom of God cannot let even the smallest item escape the rule of God's loving will.

2. A mature faith focuses on God, not some idol. Immature faith leads us to worship success, or wealth, or our nationality, always something less than God himself. But these idols always distort and finally destroy human life. The universal God of all creation and all men is alone the proper focus for a mature faith.

3. A mature faith is a working faith. I mean by this that it is not a set of theories or mental abstractions. It is a living claim that makes life different.

4. A mature faith is a growing faith. Paul wrote to the Philippian church, "Not that I . . . am already perfect; but I press on. . . ." (Philippians 3:12.) The mature person never says, "I am already finished, I have arrived."

5. A mature faith is tested in experience. It has proved itself reliable in the lives of many persons and in the life of the man of faith himself. In this testing many changes take place, but they are changes that deepen faith. They do not change faith; they make it more itself.

6. A mature faith has room for doubts. (S/R, 77.) Faith is a kind of certainty, but it is not cocksureness. It encourages the exploration of doubts in the confidence that at the end faith will be stronger and better for having examined itself more closely. Only the fanatic dares not examine his faith. Fanaticism is too unsure of itself underneath to allow any questions to be raised.

7. A mature faith gives guidance and power to life. It informs our conscience and gives moral guidance. But it does more, it gives us the power to perform what we know must be done. In this it is more than high ideals. It gives the power to love and the courage to suffer.

The kind of faith we *have* and the kind of person we *are* go together. We cannot attain to personal maturity on a kindergarten faith or no faith at all. The very nature of being human—projected as we are toward an unknown future—requires faith for our fulfillment. A wrong faith will steer us away from our true selves. A tested and mature Christian faith is the greatest aid to human maturity that is available to us.

■ Consider each of the above characteristics of a mature faith in light of First Corinthians 13. How might this Scripture enable you to move toward the kind of faith described above?

NEGATIVE CONCERNS

Another way of seeing the relationship of identity (understanding who we are) to faith is to consider the negative side. Recall that negative concerns are those things that we flee from, that we want to escape. Paul Tillich tells us that there are three of them: guilt, anxiety, and meaninglessness. These three things tend to afflict all human beings. They are not just our concerns, but the concerns of every man. They are universal.

The reason they are universal is that they are rooted in our humanity. How is this so?

Guilt. Guilt arises from two sources. The first source is the things that we have done that we ought not to have done or the things we have left undone that we ought to have done. We all recognize this kind of guilt.

But the second source of guilt arises from something deeper than sins of commission or omission. It arises from the fact that we are not the persons God intends us to be. It comes from the sense of *being* wrong, not just having *done* wrong. God implants in us the deep longing to be a son of God. But we have somehow gone astray from that goal—which is our true self.

This guilt is the underside of the longing for maturity.

Anxiety. Anxiety also arises from two sources. The first source is the natural fear of bad things that may happen to us. We may lose our job or our children may not turn out as we had hoped. We may fear illness or war.

The second source of anxiety comes from deeper levels. It is due to the fact that as human beings we are finite. That is, we are limited in wisdom and power. We are frail, subject to defeat and death. We have been given the freedom to choose what our lives shall become. This very freedom makes us anxious, because every decision we must make opens up the possibility of making a mistake.

To be anxious then seems to be one of the characteristics of being human. Anxiety seasons every hour of our lives.

Meaninglessness. We can note two kinds of meaninglessness just as we noted two kinds of guilt and anxiety. The first is the meaninglessness that comes from not finding any immediate purpose in what we are doing; say, for instance, that we are in a monotonous job, or that we are involved in an endless round of pointless recreational activities. (*S/R, 78.*)

The second and deeper kind of meaninglessness comes from a failure to find any meaning to life itself. Satisfying one's hunger by eating is meaningful. But what is the meaning of sustaining life if life itself does not have any point?

■ The negative concerns are the subject of Bulletin Board Display IV (Resource Packet, item 2). Study the pictures and the Scripture carefully before you attempt to answer the accompanying question. See the Leaders' Guide in the packet for suggestions for preparing the display and additional questions for discussion.

Study of this subject would take on additional interest if individual class members, in preparing for this session, looked in magazines and newspapers for illustrations of guilt, anxiety, and meaninglessness that are identifiable to them. They might bring these to class, tell why they chose them, and add them to the display.

FAITH AND OUR NEGATIVE CONCERNS

Faith is the answer to all three of these negative concerns. Jesus reminds us that the love of God is not limited by our forgetfulness or our misdoings. If we, like the Prodigal Son, have gone off into a far country, the Father is still waiting for us to come to ourselves. His love is greater than our guilt. His forgiveness is unlimited if we, like the Prodigal Son, accept responsibility for the mistakes we have made and resolve to act as sons.

Faith's answer to guilt is this total acceptance of the sinner by God. If we can respond by accepting God's openness toward us, then our guilt is taken away. We are restored to the family of love. We can begin again to move toward our destiny as sons.

Faith is also the answer to our anxiety. The moment we accept the fact that we are frail finite beings, that we are not gods, then we can turn to the true God for help. When we turn to him, we discover that his love supports and sustains us. As our understanding of this love deepens—and remember it is the sovereign love of the omnipotent God who created and sustains the world—our anxiety diminishes.

Jesus reminds us that God counts the very hairs of our heads. Not even a sparrow falls without his notice. And how much more valuable we human beings are in his sight! We really have nothing to fear if we trust our lives to him. Our anxiety is swallowed up in his all-powerful love.

And what about meaninglessneess? There is no answer except in faith. The atheist Jean-Paul Sartre says that man is a "useless passion." His life is wasted in futility because there is no God. But to the person who takes the incarnational faith of the New Testament seriously there is an answer.

The answer is that under God every person has a meaning for his life. Who but God could give to all the millions of human individuals a satisfactory meaning for existence? Our faith is that he does give us a purpose. And this purpose is not some general abstract purpose but a particular one. Our purpose is worked out in the details of our individual existence. That is the reason why I cannot state here what your purpose is. But God can communicate that purpose to each of us.

We begin by obeying God in this or that decision and by trusting his guidance in small details. Then as we co-operate with him over the years, a master plan tends to grow and become clearer. Often we cannot see it unless we look back. Then we can sometimes see its outlines in the tangled course of events. (S/R, 79.)

■ Work in groups of three or four persons. Silently scan the preceding section. Then one person may read aloud as others follow S/R, 79.

Now, share what you conceive to be the outline of a master plan that you discern for your life. What standards or guidelines helped you to come to this knowledge? What do you feel to be your responsibility in such a plan? What, if any, difficulties do you have with this idea of a master plan?

FAITH IN THE MODERN WORLD

The application of these truths in the modern world has become difficult for many reasons. As our little neighborhoods have become involved in the course of world events and as we see ourselves caught up with great powers and billions of persons, it seems to us that it is harder to maintain hold on the faith I have been describing.

But this is really a matter of imagination. The world has always been large. Since civilization appeared, persons have suffered the disasters of famine and war. It is just that today we read about these things in our daily papers. The faith of yesterday is still valid. Only it requires a more conscious gesture of our own to appropriate it for ourselves.

The purpose of this course of study is in part an effort to help us all enlarge our faith so that it can measure up to the size and complexity of life in the twentieth century. Our conception of God has been too small. (S/R, 80.) Our Christ and our church have been too limited. Now is the time to see that this smallness and limitation is our own doing. God and his Christ are indeed large enough to speak to the needs of modern men. The world cannot outgrow its creator, nor the Lord whom he appointed as the revelation of his purposes for the world.

We must grow up into faith. We have often allowed it to remain undeveloped and immature. Like all growing, this may be somewhat painful. But again, like growing, its fruit is the mastery of maturity. With a mature faith, we can live again.

■ Read *S/R*, 80. Let individuals share with the class the images they had, as a child, of God and Christ. Then let them say how those images have changed as they have matured. Can a growing Christian's concepts of God and Christ ever reach a point of no change? Why? Why not?

■ Pray together as a benediction, "God Be in My Head" (Resource Packet, item 1).

■ Let the leadership team be prepared to give assignments for the next chapter of study and the members of the group be prepared to accept the assignments.

NOTES ON CHAPTER 8

Pages 121-22: Martin Buber, *The Way of Man* (Wilcox and Follett Company, 1951), pages 32-33. Used by permission.

Pages 128-29: "The Criteria of Emotional Maturity," copyright 1965 by The Menninger Foundation.

REPRINTED FROM THINK MAGAZINE © 1966 IBM

Can men of faith be indifferent to the way public questions are being answered?

Let Judgement run down as waters and
righteousness as a mighty stream — Amos 2 4

but the Lord of hosts shall be exalted in
judgment, and God that is holy shall be
sanctified in righteousness.
Isaiah 5:16

Read these selections in your Bible:
Amos 5:21-24
True religion as justice.

Isaiah 3:13-26; 5:7-9, 16
The Lord judges Israel for her lack of social justice.

9

□□□

A THEOLOGY OF
SOCIAL CONCERN

"Thousands of years ago, the Egyptians believed that no soul could justify itself after death unless it could say, 'I have never let any one suffer from hunger.' All Christians know they are liable to hear Christ Himself say to them one day, 'I was an hungered, and ye gave me no meat.' " *

"O Thou who art heroic love: Keep alive in our hearts that adventurous spirit which makes men scorn the way of safety, so that thy will may be done. For so only, O Lord, shall we be worthy of those courageous souls, who in every age have ventured all in obedience to thy call, and for whom

---

■ *As you arrive at your place of meeting, check the assignment chart for specific preparation to be made before the session begins.*
■ *Set goals for your study of this chapter as suggested on page 16.*

the trumpets have sounded on the farther shore; through Jesus Christ our Lord." *

*   *   *

One reason why Protestantism has not been able to deal effectively with social problems in America is that it has had no convincing theology of social concern. Action on social questions has usually been limited to alcoholic beverages, gambling, and Sunday observance. Most of the pressing social questions are left aside to be considered entirely from secular points of view. (S/R, 81 and 82.)

This attitude has not always been the case with our faith. The great prophets of the Old Testament envisioned a society totally renovated and ruled by God. Amos spoke out against corrupt courts, the callousness of the rich, and wars of aggression. Isaiah was as concerned with the conservation of his country's resources as he was with the reform of worship. Jeremiah was imprisoned for his preaching on foreign policy.

■ Have a symposium based on S/R, 81, 82 and 83. Let three persons, selected in advance, be prepared to present short speeches on the subject of social concern and the church. Each speaker will use one of the selected readings as a basis for his presentation. He will also need to gather additional information. Each speaker might climax his talk by characterizing the viewpoint of his reading in a key sentence.

Let the members of the class discuss each point of view apart from the selected reading. As background for the discussion, have three persons read aloud Amos 5:21-24; Isaiah 3:13-26; and Isaiah 5:7-9, 16.

WHY WE LACK A THEOLOGY OF SOCIAL CONCERN

The early church tended to forget the social implications of the message of Jesus and interpret the gospel in personal terms. This personal emphasis may have resulted in part from reaction to the Old Testament emphasis on the nation and the community of God's people. The personal emphasis was also, no doubt, the result of the disillusionment of the Jews with history. With every crisis the Jews faced, the promise of achieving the social ideals of the Old Testament seemed to get further away.

By the time of Jesus it seemed clear that the efforts of good men would not bring about the ideal society foretold by Isaiah. Only God could do that. So the concept of a good society was postponed, so to speak, to a time beyond history when God would intervene to set things right.

In this setting the early church emphasized God's unlimited concern for individuals. It held out a promise of personal salvation for all who came to the faith. This concern for persons was, of course, necessary, as we shall see, for any truly Christian view of the social scene. But it was also a reflection of the fact that the early church was too small to change the power structures of society. Furthermore, most of its converts were among the social outcasts of ancient society.

The great ideal of the Kingdom slumbered only to be awakened in later thought.

After the fourth century, the church was no longer a small poverty-stricken minority. It grew in wealth and social power. It became in time responsible for the entire social order: crowning princes, regulating trade, initiating legal changes, and controlling education.

During this period—what we call the Middle Ages—the church had a theology for society as a whole. It was a theology for a total Catholic Christian culture. Every part of medieval society reflected Catholic religious values. Marriage, for instance, was made into a sacrament and divorce was outlawed.

■ Let us assume that the text is right in saying that the central message of Jesus was the kingdom of God. Compare a hymn of personal salvation ("Ask Ye What Great Thing I Know," *The Methodist Hymnal*, 124 or "Blessed Assurance, Jesus Is Mine," *The Methodist Hymnal*, 224) with one about social action ("Lord, Whose Love Through Humble Service," *The Methodist Hymnal*, 479 or

"O Young and Fearless Prophet," *The Methodist Hymnal,* 173).
Which in your opinion is closer Jesus' idea of the kingdom of God?
Why?

THE REFORMATION RETURNS TO PRIVATE CONCERNS

After a thousand years of Catholic culture, the Reformation returned Protestant Europe to predominantly private concerns. Faith concerned itself with the private sphere of individual salvation. Changes in state and economic life were to be left to the secular authorities, according to the views of Martin Luther. The individual lived, as it were, in two worlds—the secular world and the world of faith.

This is, of course, an oversimplification. The change did not take place at once. Some Protestants, such as Calvin and our New England forefathers, tried to establish ideal Christian communities based upon a theology of social concern. But these efforts were abandoned by the churches in favor of a purely personal type of religion. In the late 1600's, the movement known as "pietism" arose in Germany and spread to England and America. Pietism emphasized personal religious experience, though pietists did establish orphanages and schools.

Can faith be satisfied with a theology of individual salvation? A missionary tells about his own conversion to social action after years in the field. Year after year, he said, he baptized infants in villages only to return a few months later to find three fourths of them dead from preventable disease. Any sane man would have questioned whether he had done all he could for these people in the name of Christ as long as this situation continued.

He collected funds from the people at home to dig cesspools in the villages. The death rate of babies dropped. Instead of dead babies, he had live Christians. But the church at home wondered about his use of missionary funds.

The connection between individual religious welfare and

the social order is not always so evident. However, the story has a lesson for us: We dare not ignore the concrete conditions of a man's life if we really want to help his soul. Certainly our Lord did not refuse to help people in this way. What has this to do with a theology of social concerns? What are the forces that most powerfully shape our lives today? Are they not the major institutions of society? What affects a man and his family more than unemployment or being drafted into a shooting war? If we are honest, do we not discover that the economic and political system we live under tends almost irresistibly to shape our attitudes and deeds—in short, our lives?

Can Christianity claim to give guidance for men in the twentieth century if it is silent on these major public questions? Can we be indifferent as men of faith to the way public questions are being answered?

■ Listen as two persons, assigned in advance, discuss aloud for five to eight minutes, what it means to live in "one" world. The conversation might deal with questions such as: What is meant by a secular world and a world of faith? Do two such worlds exist for us? If so, why do they come into existence? What attitudes and actions are reserved for the secular world? for the world of faith? What difference would be made in our way of living if we truly lived in "one" world?

Allow time for class members to react.

■ Let the class state what they consider to be one of the major social problems in society today, such as the population explosion, unemployment, racial injustice. Several may be suggested from which the class may choose one.

Now proceed in this fashion: (1) Write the problem at the top of the chalkboard or a sheet of newsprint. (2) Divide the chalkboard or newsprint into two columns. Label the left column "Pro" and the right column "Con." (3) In the left column list all the factors that your class can think of that might help in solving the problem. (4) In the right column list the forces working against solution of the problem.

Now, divide the class into two groups, those who will work on the "pro" factors and those on the "con" forces. Smaller units within these two groups may be formed if your class is large. Discuss: How can we use these factors/forces to work toward elimination of the problem? What steps can we take?

Allow time for a report from each group. You may wish to make plans to implement your suggested action.

A THEOLOGY OF SOCIAL CONCERN——THE RESPONSIBLE SOCIETY

The term *the responsible society* was formulated in the First Assembly of the World Council of Churches in 1948. The Assembly was made up of people from many countries with many different social and economic systems. Some common understanding of the claims of the gospel on to-day's society was needed. It obviously could not be a concept taken over from any one national group.

Here is what the Assembly finally agreed upon: "A responsible society is one where freedom is the freedom of men who acknowledge responsibility to justice and public order, and where those who hold political authority or economic power are responsible for its exercise to God and the people whose welfare is affected by it." *

Broadly speaking, four views of society compete for men's allegiance today. The first tells us that men are merely self-centered social atoms. Society, according to this view, should leave them alone in their economic and social activities. This view fits into a theology that asks the church to leave the social order alone and concern itself solely with the souls of individuals. (S/R, 83.)

A second view of society tells us that the social order is of primary importance. Individuals must serve society. This is the philosophy of compulsory collectivism that we saw in Germany under Hitler and see today in Russia and other Marxist societies.

A third view of society is held by humanistic reformers who feel that man's social environment should help him develop toward a more "ideal" person. Its major appeal is often to the self-interest of persons. It says, in effect, if you want to help yourself, help others.

The fourth view is the Christian concept of a responsible society. It rejects the first three views as either false or partial. The Christian faith, with its teaching of love for one's neighbor, proclaims that men belong to one another. Like Christ, Christians are to live for others. The appeal is not to selfishness but to sacrifice. Society should be directed toward aiding —not hindering—men to develop as sons of God. Anything that affects another person is within the sphere of Christian concern. Management practices in corporations, zoning a city, political campaigns, and wage policies are examples of the legitimate sphere of Christian concern.

The Christian view of society, then, is of a true community in which men are concerned for one another's welfare. It is not content to deal with men's souls alone but with everything that either builds them up or tears them down as human beings.

■ Let one half of the class brainstorm (list without discussion) situations, attitudes, conditions that build men up as human beings. The other half of the class should brainstorm situations, attitudes, conditions that tear men down as human beings. Each group should keep a record of its work on newsprint or chalkboard.

Now, in the total group, ask this question about each item listed: How has the church contributed to this situation, attitude, or condition?

A theology of Christian society will put first this question: *Are we reflecting God's concern for human beings?* The World Council Assembly in 1948 said this: "Man must never be made a mere means for political or economic ends. Man is not made for the State but the State for man. Man is not made for production, but production for man." * This is an echo of our Lord's saying, "The sabbath was made for man, not man for the sabbath." (Mark 2:27.)

A leading theologian today answers the question, "What is

143

God doing?" in this way. He says, God is working to "keep human life human." *

The whole purpose of creation, according to the New Testament, is to bring to birth the sons of God, to bring the human race up to the fullness of life that was manifested in Jesus Christ. The aim of any good society is to create the conditions under which human beings can grow toward that end. Of course, conditions do not guarantee that a person will grow in this direction. Becoming a Christian is an individual choice. But a man who really wants a favorable setting for growth to take place in the Christian life cannot be indifferent to schools, jobs, housing, and the like. Men are often warped in mind and spirit by a diseased social setting just as much as they are warped in body. War, poverty, ignorance, disease, social humiliation, bitter strife—these are powerful forces that must be the concern of Christians who would obey their Lord in the twentieth century. (*S/R,* 84.)

■ Have a research team share articles or pictures they have found in newspapers or magazines to illustrate the four views of society discussed above. (The team should be chosen in the preceding session since they will probably need to meet during the week to prepare the assignment.) Pages 4-7 of *Adult Teacher,* June, July, August, 1968, may be of help. Team members should tell how each article illustrates a particular view of society.

Discuss in the total group: How prevalent is each view? At what points do any or all of these views touch your life?

■ Study *S/R,* 84. Discuss the possibilities for implementing the plan suggested in the reading. You may wish to unite efforts with other adult classes in your church school. Perhaps a committee could explore with your pastor possible ways of proceeding and report back to your group.

IS CHRISTIANITY UTOPIAN?

For centuries, men have dreamed of ideal societies. We call these utopias.

A theology of a responsible society is not utopian. It is a theology for men who live here and now in this world.

144

The Christian does not expect to achieve a perfect society. Nor does he imagine that ideals have a way of automatically becoming fact. This theology asks us to take seriously the concrete work of social change that is possible here and now. It does not live by the illusion that men can by their own efforts bring in the kingdom of God.

The trouble with living by the illusion that society can be made perfect is that after a while one becomes *dis*illusioned. Then cynicism takes over.

Christian theology recognizes that men are less than perfect. It acknowledges that they are sinners and that this sin will not disappear automatically under good social conditions. In fact, men tend to corrupt every situation in which they find themselves.

Only the grace of God can save men from sin. Only the love of God can turn men from themselves outward toward their neighbor's need. No man ever gets beyond the need of grace. In any social order that we can imagine, the church has a gospel for individual men as well as for the social order. This gospel is the salt that keeps the whole social order from decay and corruption. We must consider further the role of the church in the next chapter.

A responsible society will prize freedom. It will seek to create the conditions in which men may exercise their freedom. In this sense the Christian will work to humanize those forces that tend to take away men's freedom. I mean such things as war, unemployment, enforced life in a city slum, and so on. He will work to make effective our American tradition of individual rights.

However, freedom "from" is never enough. There must be freedom "for" something that makes human existence more noble. Our work for a responsible society is only half done when we have labored on behalf of freeing men from degrading social forces. We then have to engage in the hard work of education and enlightenment. We have to create opportunities for men to learn to think and to love according to the pattern of Christ. This is the educational task for the family, the school, and the church.

Freedom "from" and freedom "for" have another counterpart: freedom "with." Freedom "with" is what we mean by democracy. To be truly free means that men have a share in making the decisions by which they must live. A man who lives entirely by the rules of another is not yet a full man. At best he is a child; at worse, a slave. He cannot grow up until he participates in his own government. (S/R, 85.)

In this broad sense, a theology of social concern favors some kind of democratic social life. This is what the Amsterdam Assembly meant by saying that political and economic power are responsible to the people whose welfare is affected by it.

We must be careful not to think that a society must be like America to be Christian. The varied social circumstances of the world make that very unrealistic. It does mean, however, that democracy is in some sense a part of God's work today in making and keeping human life human. And we will not have understood the meaning of this American experiment until we understand the meaning of power "with" in contrast to power "over."

History is full of societies that demonstrated the evil effects of a government of the few in their power "over" the many. One of the advantages of our present-day perspective is that we can see the flaw in that kind of social life.

Christians have taught that love is greater than justice, and they are right. But love without justice is mere sentimentality. Treating human beings justly is the social foundation for bringing them to an understanding of love. To say that you love a man whom you underpay in your factory or whom you refuse to associate with because of his color is not Christian love. It is sentimentality. It tries to "paper over" the large question of elementary justice.

Christians in a responsible society must also be concerned

with physical needs. For years missionaries have discovered that service to these needs—health, education, and food production, for instance—is one of the best ways to make men receptive to the Christian message. Some people have accused the missionaries of trying to buy converts. This is a false interpretation. They were simply aware of the fact that you cannot talk meaningfully to starving people of the love of Christ unless you try to help them find food for their bodies.

> ■ Group discussion: In light of the above discussion what, from the Christian view, is wrong with the statement, "Those who 'own' (pay for) the country should have the right to govern it"? See S/R, 85. What is your church doing to support efforts at self-help among the poor? To influence public opinion in support of involvement of the poor in solving their problems? How are your attitudes and actions reflecting God's concern for individuals?

THE MEANING OF THE TWENTIETH CENTURY

When the Christian faith is true to its Lord, it is always prophetic. The prophetic sense is the power to discern the true meaning of a given historical period. An adequate social theology requires an interpretation of the meaning of our century, the "signs of the times." Though it shares common features with past history, our time is also unique in many respects. This uniqueness suggests that God is at work doing new things.

Consider some of the facts: Science has created a system of world-wide communication that can put everyone in touch with the whole human community. We can sit at our television sets and see men fighting in the jungles of Vietnam. News of every small crisis is instantly sent throughout the world. The nervous system of a world community is coming into existence.

New independent nations are being formed out of the old colonial regions of the world. Everywhere human beings are demanding the right to self-determination, the freedom to rule themselves, even if they do it badly. Freedom is a theme of present-day history.

The colored peoples of the world are insisting upon an equal dignity with the dominant white populations of the West. They will no longer tolerate being second-class citizens of the world. Equality is another theme in the events of our age. (S/R, 86.)

Most of these rising new colored nations are also bent on the abolition of poverty and disease through economic development. They demand a share of the earth's wealth that has traditionally gone to the dominant nations. A broader economic justice is their claim thunderously proclaimed in the councils of the world.

As these things proceed, the world population is growing at a fantastic rate. Populations equal to whole nations are added to the world each year. This has led to a crisis in food production in some countries and has given terrible urgency to the task of agricultural development. It also lends urgency to finding means for population control.

The new kind of society that is emerging in response to these demands is predominantly a city culture. Human beings are more and more leaving the land, their small villages, and towns to dwell in huge metropolises. (S/R, 87.) Millions in these cities have found themselves cut off from their ancestral roots and huddled together in indescribable slums.

These changes have all been accompanied by a new level of violence. The twentieth century is already the bloodiest of twenty-five centuries of Western history. It has killed proportionately and in absolute numbers more human beings than all previous centuries added together.

These are undisputed facts of our age. What do they mean?

Many people who are frightened by these changes believe that they are the work of evil forces bent on destroying the foundations of the past. These people are panicked by change. It seems to me, however, that God is working through these

148

changes to elevate the lives of his children all around the world. Perhaps we cannot help being anxious about these massive changes for they require new ways of thinking and acting. We are not always sure that we will be equal to the demands upon us. Some persons denounce the supposedly evil forces that are making change inevitable in the name of the Christian faith. I think that they are wrong. The Christian knows that God moves mysteriously and powerfully in history. (See again S/R, 1.)

I believe that God is doing things in our century that have never been done before and that the Christian faith should be on the growing edge of these changes. The changes are violent, because they are resisted instead of encouraged and guided.

It would be naïve, of course, to say that every proposed change is the will of God. Man's judgment is always subject to error. As I have already said, however, the primary concern of Christians when facing change is: "Will this change help persons?" If the answer is yes, the Christian's responsibility is clear.

■ Read silently the preceding section. Then let each person respond in turn to any or all of these items: (1) Tell where and how any one of the changes listed above has actually changed your living patterns. (2) How has your mental image of or feeling toward persons in another part of the world (India, China, Japan, Russia, Africa, and the like) changed within the last five years? What does this change mean to you?

THE UNIT IS HUMANITY

One of the things that God is doing today is making a world-community out of mankind. In the past we have thought about nations or even civilizations as units. But now the only real unit is humanity. The globe itself has to be considered as the sphere of our actions. We cannot be content to consider the effects of our actions on our own race or na-

149

tion or civilization. The effects of our actions spread outward to the world, just as the ripples in a pond spread outward to every shore.

The Christian task is still the same as it was when Paul announced it in his letter to the Corinthian church (2 Corinthians 5:18) —reconciliation. If we have indeed been reconciled to God by the manifestation of his love in Jesus Christ, then we have a ministry to all mankind to reconcile them to God and to one another. This task will take many forms, but its aim will be reconciling person to person, race to race, and nation to nation. (S/R, 88.)

What this means is no doubt some kind of responsible world order in which the great promise of twentieth-century knowledge can be used to benefit persons instead of threatening them with degradation and destruction. Without a reconciling ministry of love, the very science that could bless us will turn to a fire of judgment.

I do not believe that it is God's intention that this already bloody century is to be bathed in nuclear fire, nor that its exploding population is to be condemned to desperate hunger, nor that the pride of nations is to multiply the enmities of past history. Of course, all of these things could happen if men remain deaf to God's message of reconciliation. It is our business as Christians to see that at least this message is heard clearly and purely. It is our task to leap over the barriers of our past thoughts and prejudices and join with all whom God's spirit is moving in this strange and wonderful century. (S/R, 89.)

■ Evaluate: What new understandings have you gained in this session? How will those understandings help as you attempt to reinterpret the faith this week?

■ Read in unison the Korean Creed, The Methodist Hymnal, 741, as a benediction or use "God Be in My Head" (Resource Packet, item 1).

■ Let the leadership team be prepared to give assignments for the next chapter of study and the members of the group be prepared to accept the assignments.

NOTES ON CHAPTER 9

Page 137: Simone Weil, *The Need for Roots* (Beacon Press, 1955), page 6. Copyright 1952 by G. P. Putnam's Sons. Used by permission.

Page 137-38: *The Book of Worship* (The Methodist Publishing House, 1964), page 246, number 13. Copyright © 1964, 1965 by Board of Publication of The Methodist Church. Used by permission.

Page 142: Quoted in *Man's Disorder and God's Design* (Harper and Row, 1949), volume 3, page 200. Used by permission.

Page 143: Quoted in *Man's Disorder and God's Design,* volume 3, page 200. Used by permission.

Page 143-44: Paul L. Lehmann, *Ethics in a Christian Context* (Harper and Row, 1963), page 124. Copyright © 1963 by Paul L. Lehmann. Used by permission.

LAWRENCE COPES

*Secular man
can do God's will
in a secular society.*

Read these selections in your Bible:
Galatians 3:28
No race or caste in Christ.

Revelation 4:1-6, 8-11
Only God is to be worshiped as God.

Ephesians 4:7, 11-14
A task for each and each to his task.

10
□□□

THE GOSPEL AND
SOCIAL INSTITUTIONS

"By virtue of the Creation and, still more, of the Incarnation, *nothing* here below is *profane* for those who know how to see." *

*   *   *

What have theology and social institutions to do with each other? The gospel deals with "religion," and social institutions belong to the secular side of life; at least, so some say. (*S/R*, 90.)

In this chapter I want to apply some of the ideas of the previous chapter to five social institutions: the family, business, state, education, and the church.

■ *As you arrive at your place of meeting, check the assignment chart for specific preparation to be made before the session begins.*
■ *Set goals for your study of this chapter as suggested on page 16.*

The Bible is not "religious" in the sense that many people would like to believe; what I mean is that only a small proportion of space in the Bible is given to instruction on specifically "religious" activities like worship or prayer. Much more space is given to "nonreligious" topics such as economics, politics, foreign affairs, family life, and so on. The conclusion we come to is that the Bible is concerned with the whole of life, not with some compartment of life labeled "religion."

God is the God of the whole of life. He is more pleased by acts of justice and a kingdom justly ruled than by a new temple built in his honor.

If you read the description of the New Jerusalem in the last book of the Bible, you will discover that there is no church there, no temple. (Revelation 21:22.) The reason is that the whole of life has been brought into perfect obedience to God. God's concern is not a pure "religion" but a holy society. That society would be one in which all the spheres of life—family, politics, economics, and culture—are governed entirely by reverence for human life.

This vision of the New Jerusalem seems to mean that the goal of God's work with man is not a church but a new society, a totally new kind of human community.

Some recent thinkers have suggested that for this reason the church is not important as an institution and that the Bible not only approves but fosters a secularization of human society. Such a secularization has been going on for the last three hundred years in Western civilization, and it is now spreading around the world. (*S/R,* 91.) Religion *as such* seems to have less and less importance in the lives of nations.

These thinkers do not regret this. They believe that man has "come of age," to use a phrase of the German theologian Dietrich Bonhoeffer who was martyred by Hitler. They claim that Christians are mistaken to concern themselves with "religion." What God wants is secular men who do his will in secular society.

What they propose is a new secular life under God. They call it "worldly holiness" or "religionless Christianity." They claim that Christianity is not a *religion* at all. It is *the life of faith*. The notion that Christianity is a religion, they say, has led to a kind of "church-ianity" that has obscured the biblical teaching of God's sovereignty over the whole of life.

These writers are emphasizing a great truth of the Bible, perhaps the most important one. For if we identify God's sphere of activity with the church alone, we deny him as the creator of the world and the Lord of history. (*S/R*, 92.) They point out, quite rightly, I believe, that if we do not recover this faith in God's dominion over the secular regions of life, Christianity will continue to diminish in influence. It will become a hobby for the small minority of men who happen to be interested in "religion."

Earlier in this book, I have spoken of "doing theology." "Doing" in this phrase emphasizes that theology is more than having correct theological ideas; "doing" means that our genuine religious beliefs are seen in what we do as well as in what we think. "Doing theology" means then that we must put our beliefs to work; when we are "doing theology," we are developing and carrying out a plan of action to fulfill the will of God in the world.

If, then, we are to be faithful to the Bible, and if we are sincere in our aim of "doing theology," we cannot fail to think deeply about a theology for social institutions. We must ask what God's will is for the family, school, state, and economic system.

■ In groups of four to six persons study scriptural passages that deal with the priority of justice: Isaiah 1:10-17; 58:1-12; Amos 5:14-15, 21-24; Micah 6:8; Matthew 23:23.

How would the injunctions in these passages contribute toward a society governed by reverence for human life?

Each group might select one passage and paraphrase (put into your own words) it, making it speak to situations in contemporary society. See S/R, 22 in God With Us as an example of paraphrasing. Allow time for groups to share their paraphrased passages.

■ In the total group discuss: Why do people assume that God is active only in the church? What are signs or marks of his presence? Have one person read aloud S/R, 92. What clues to discerning signs of God's presence do you find in the reading?

Now, in pairs, work out some signs by which people have thought they could discern God. For example, some say God is active wherever men are coming to understand each other. What statements could you make? What do these scriptural passages say about where God can be seen at work: Genesis 33; 45:4-15; Acts 8:26-40; 16:6-10; 2 Corinthians 5:16-21? What criteria do you use for arriving at your statements? Allow time to hear brief reports from teams.

■ On the basis of the above definition of "doing theology," what does it mean to "do theology" in relation to the five social institutions discussed in this chapter—family, business, state, education, and the church?

GOD AND THE FAMILY

The family is humanity's basic institution. From it each new generation arises. And in its intimate warmth the new generation is nurtured during the tender age when teaching has its most lasting effects. Long before the school sees him, the child has been molded by the family in ways that can never be wholly changed.

But what light can Christian theology shed on the family? There can be no doubt of its importance to religion. The New Testament draws a parallel between the marriage bond and the relationship between Christ and his church. But the parallel only has meaning if marriage is itself interpreted as a personal, loving, and totally caring relationship between the sexes. (S/R, 93.) Faith teaches that a marriage based upon undisciplined sexual lust is destructive of both the individuals involved and the community itself.

This is why marriage is conceived as a kind of sacrament. It is the purification of the human race at its very source. The human family is part of God's intention for man. He made humanity sexed. The story of creation says that God looked upon this as very good. Man's sin is not rooted in his sexuality but in his pride. It is man turning inward upon himself as the center of life that perverts not only his sex life but his entire response to existence.

The reformer John Calvin wrote that the sexual act is "undefiled, honorable and holy, because it is a pure institution of God." * It is human selfishness that has corrupted the sphere of man's sexuality. God intends in his grace to restore that function to its original innocence. This claim stands against a very long and mistaken Christian notion that there is something wrong or unholy about sex as such.

The family is a sexual institution, but it cannot be understood simply as a relationship between a man and a woman. If the intimate relations between husband and wife can be inspired by God's real intention, then the next step is to inspire them with a tender regard for their offspring.

Children are the human future. In this sense parents do not own their children. They hold them in trust for God and humanity. In their most impressionable years they have the primary responsibility to lead them into a life of faith and love. This means, of course, religious training of some sort. But it means much more a healthy and loving environment in which the child learns what human life is at its intimate best. A child who is wanted, loved, and even reverenced as humanity's growing edge has by far the best chance to grow up into a mature adult.

We recognize, of course, that a family is not always two parents and small children. In our society, there are many other family groupings. When we talk about the family, we may mean one parent and dependent children, elderly parents and a grown unmarried son or daguhter who live in the same household, and the like.

From the point of view of theology, the family can be thought of as the "smallest of local churches . . . the church in miniature." *

The social forces of modern life are massively arrayed against the family. (S/R, 94.) Many of its past functions have been progressively taken away from it by other institutions. A century ago in America the family was the major center for economic, recreational, and educational activity. Now these functions are performed impersonally elsewhere.

Furthermore, as more families move into giant cities, the environment for rearing children becomes less and less favorable because children are exposed to harsh and impersonal influences at a very early age. The great task of healing the family requires that we make our cities places of human habitation instead of ant heaps of economic striving. We have to labor, writes John Macquarrie, for the "maintenance of personal values and for the supreme importance of love in a world where these are gravely threatened." * Christians must seek ways to reconcile the degrading influences in every aspect of family life.

■ Examine the concept of family life and family roles in popular television programs or series. What do the programs depict as typical contemporary family life? What is the image of the father, mother, child, teen-agers? What conscious or unconscious theological assumptions underlie the story line of the shows? How do they contribute to the strengthening of family life? or to the disintegration of family?

Members of the class may individually view at least one, possibly more, TV shows built around family roles or family life during the week prior to this session. Or you might plan an additional session when the entire class will view one or more shows together. Group discussion should follow either of those approaches.

■ Perhaps your group will want to invite a representative from one of the community agencies related to family life and needs to speak to your group. Persons responsible for making the arrangements would talk with the representative about the specific subject you would like to hear discussed.

■ Discuss: The text says that the social forces of modern life are arrayed against the family. What are these social forces? How are they working against the family? What, if any, positive benefits do they offer? How might the church tend to split the family rather than bring members together? What steps can be taken to avoid this?

A THEOLOGY OF GOVERNMENT

Government has become increasingly a part of our lives. This is not only true in America. It is a dominant fact of life everywhere in the world. We might wish that government would somehow "go away," but the forces of modern history all tend to make it more and more indispensable. We are more sensible, then, to ask what kind of government God wants and to try to obey his will in our political life.

We have already covered many important points on this subject in the previous chapter. The message of the Amsterdam Assembly makes the primary point: The state must be responsible to God and to the people whose welfare it deals with. In American terms, this means a democratic government concerned with human welfare.

There are two sides to this truth. One side is the role of government in helping people to help themselves in those areas of life in which private institutions cannot succeed. There is no rule for deciding in advance just what those areas are. One area, for example, which most Americans now agree requires governmental action is retirement income. Social security permits people in middle and lower income brackets to save for their retirement years.

Other governmental functions are still disputed. Theology does not help us settle these disputes. It merely sets forth the principle that the welfare of the people is a proper function of government under modern conditions. For it is these modern conditions that prevent men from solving some issues of their welfare apart from governmental action.

How the welfare of the people is to be cared for is a subject of disagreement in our society. The lively debate on just where the lines are to be drawn is healthy. (*S/R*, 95, 96, and 97.) Generally speaking, it is better for men to develop private solutions to their problems wherever possible instead of turning automatically to government. Governments have a way of interfering with personal freedoms.

Another truth that theology must underscore is the importance of human rights. Many of these rights place a limit on the interference of government with human freedoms. If governments exist for the people, then there are limits to government. Or to put it another way: One of the purposes of government is to build barriers against political or economic forces that take away human freedom.

Part of the struggle for rights means to put limits on oppressive government activity. We do not want government officials to arbitrarily enter its citizens' homes or arrest them without due cause, or to tell them how to worship, or to take away their property.

But we must also recognize that, for instance, an unemployed man who really wants to work cannot be said to be really free. If the private sector of the economy cannot provide such work, most Americans believe that the government should be concerned. Again, it is debatable just how that concern should show itself. But the demand for political action is still valid. Christians must thoughtfully look at the functions of government to discover ways in which politics aid and hinder the development of persons into their full humanity.

■ The administration of the welfare of people is the subject of much disagreement. Let three persons be prepared to read aloud *S/R*, 95, 96, and 97. Each reader should be prepared to make two or three brief statements supporting the premise of his reading. Then let the class divide into three groups. Each group will react to one of the readings. If your class is large, more than one group may deal with the same reading. When time is called, each group should be prepared to report why they agree or why they disagree with the premise of their reading.

■ Theology stresses the importance of human rights. Have one person interview a lawyer prior to this session on this subject: What rights belong to man simply because he is a man? Hear the report of the interviewer. What, if any, scriptural basis can class members see for the views expressed in the interview?

A THEOLOGY FOR BUSINESS

In the nineteenth century, most Americans thought that business was business and should be let alone by both church and state. After the great depression of the 1930's, this view gradually faded as a majority view. During the depression, businessmen begged the government to "do something." It became apparent that economic activity had too many effects upon human beings to be allowed unchecked license to go its own way. We have been painfully trying to evolve some principles that could guide honest men in their solution to these problems.

Let us take for an example a recent problem that affects everyone in America—the pollution of water and air. With the enormous growth of industry and population, the amount of filth being poured into our water and air has begun to threaten life everywhere. Clean water and air would seem to be a normal human right. It does not make sense to talk about a responsible society if these fundamental necessities for life are poisoned.

This example is important because it shows how governmental obligations change as society changes. (S/R, 98.) When industry was small and populations were scattered in small communities, pollution affected only the few. But now, as the enormous clouds of smog drift even over our deserts, and rivers and lakes become so polluted that the fish die, we are all ready to concede that rules must be enforced to reverse this wanton destruction of our life-supporting environment. Businessmen themselves are concerned about these problems. Many of them are concerned about how to reconcile the need to run a profitable business with the need to recognize the public interest. (S/R, 99.)

Theology does not tell us what actions to take, but faith in Christ makes clear the human responsibility to make and keep our environment fit for human habitation.

Business exists for people, not people for business. This principle is easily forgotten in the pursuit of personal profit. But is there any way to really deny it, if we keep the Christian concept of human life in mind? Fortunately, the business community has increasingly in recent years begun to take this idea seriously, no doubt under the prodding of events and widespread criticism.

Businessmen in conference with religious leaders agreed upon eleven goals as proper guides for business management in a Christian society.* Here is a brief summary of those goals:

1. The production of goods is primarily for the survival and well-being of all members of society.

2. Economic life should be arranged in such a way that participation in production, distribution, and consumption does not divide the commonwealth into bitter warring factions. There should be a strong sense of participation and even of fellowship on the part of each member of the economy. (See again S/R, 85.)

3. Each person should have a position that does not deprive him of human dignity. Power over others should be borne with humility as a public trust.

4. All work should contribute to, or at least be consistent with, moral and social enlightenment so that men may participate intelligently in responsible economic decisions.

5. Production and consumption should contribute not only to an abundance of goods but also should avoid making the environment ugly. If possible, it should make life's surroundings more attractive.

6. Despite the necessity for mass production, a just eco-

nomic order will provide ever-widening opportunities for creative imagination. A certain freedom for individuals to contribute to the final quality of the product they are manufacturing should be provided for.

7. Industrialism has produced widespread boredom, but a just economic order will regard variety and novelty as important goals of its activity.

8. An economic system should provide for the physical and psychological security of its members as far as its resources will permit. (See again S/R, 17 and 95.)

9. Freedom should be another goal of the economy; the progressive removal of undue external restraints.

10. The economy should move toward the day when all men will be treated with equal consideration and given the same opportunities regardless of their race, political and religious creeds, or cultural memberships.

11. The *climactic goal of an economic system is service to the personal growth of its members.* The final test of every economic institution is the kind of person it tends to produce, the quality of community life it fosters, and the level of ultimate values and meanings it encourages.

To a large degree, these goals represent a growing consensus among the Christian churches of the world—Protestant and Catholic. They represent a long step from the time when economic life was thought to be beyond the concern of the Christian faith. These guidelines offer some suggestion to the businessman in what "doing theology" may mean.

■ Have one person read aloud S/R, 98 as others follow the reading. Discuss: As a Christian citizens' group, (1) what kinds of dangers do you see in the economic and political power of the Defense Department? (2) How can this power be used in nonmilitary ways to promote justice for all persons? (3) How do you feel about the immunity of the defense budget to cutting by Congress, compared to cutting back foreign aid askings?
■ Let the total group consider the goals suggested as guides for business management. As each goal is read aloud, add the words

"which means. . . ." Then let someone try to restate the goal according to its function in a concrete situation. What theological assumptions underlie each goal?

A THEOLOGY OF EDUCATION

Every American is affected by education, either directly or indirectly. Has theology anything to say about it? If Christian faith lays any claim to giving guidance to life in the twentieth century, it should have a view of education. Unfortunately, these remarks must be too brief. But here are a few things that seem to stand out when we look at education from the perspective of Christian theology.

"The central aim of education" writes Philip H. Phenix, a leading philosopher of education, "should be the transformation of persons so that they will serve the good instead of pleasing themselves." * This aim is in harmony with the Christian faith.

The purpose of education is not merely to teach people how to read and write, or to train them for jobs, or to give them the tools for success, but to develop in them a loyalty to what is excellent. This view is very close to that of philosopher Alfred North Whitehead, who said that "the essence of education is that it be religious." * (S/R, 100.)

Since the schools are financed and run by the community as a whole, they are to this degree a governmental operation. For this reason neither sectarian religion nor acts of worship may be introduced into the classroom or assemblies. Many Christians do not understand why prayers and religious acts do not belong in the school. (S/R, 101.) They would feel differently if they were in a non-Christian community and the prayers which the children were taught were non-Christian. Then they would realize that school worship is a species of compulsory state religion.

However, it seems clear from the Supreme Court decisions that we can legally teach religion objectively in the schools.

"Objectively" means that the Bible could be studied as history and literature, including the analysis of ideas. Church history could be taught along with the history of wars and governments. Courses on these subjects would at least make students religiously literate. Knowledge gained in this way would help the churches do their own work better.

Note that teaching *about* religion is not the same thing as teaching men to be religious. The public schools should not become a battleground in which teachers try to win converts for their particular denomination or faith. Instead, emphasis should be given to the fact that neither American history nor the history of Western civilization can be fully understood apart from knowledge of the Bible and the history of the church.

A theology of education calls for education to be an instrument through which persons might discover the deeper purposes of life. For students, teachers, and administrators, as well as for all responsible citizens, the schools and educational philosophy are an area in which "doing theology" is meaningful.

■ Have a panel made up of a teacher, a senior high school boy or girl, parents of school children, and a school administrator discuss these questions: What is the purpose of education as conceived in your local school system? If Phenix and Whitehead as quoted above are right, what is the difference between religion and education?
  Allow time for class members to question and react to the panel.
■ Study the "Objective of Christian Education" (*S/R*, 100). Analyze it to answer this question: What parts of the Objective would be just as appropriate in public schools as in the church school?
■ Religion in public schools is widely debated these days. Read *S/R*, 101. How does this reading affect your attitude toward the practice of religious acts in the public schools?

A THEOLOGY OF THE CHURCH

The church is the last primary institution to be discussed. I believe that those theologians mentioned earlier in this chapter who underrate the need for a separate religious

165

institution in modern society are wrong. To be sure, in the New Jerusalem there may be no need of a temple, for there God is everything to everybody. But midway here in history things are different. The human being needs the services of a religious institution if he is to be reminded of the meaning of our common life together.

The ideal is for men to be serving God in everything they do. But this purpose easily fades away unless there are times set aside for religious instruction and worship. Just as family life needs the structures of the legal institution of marriage to protect and shelter it, so the religious life has need of the church.

The mission of the church is to make Christ evident in every area of life. It will use its preaching, teaching, and sacraments to serve this goal. It cannot do this effectively if the church is itself not a fellowship modeled on the teachings of its Lord. The church should be an institution of fellowship in which men come to know directly what the love of God means in relationship to other people. From its own institutional life, the church should develop that same quality of life—fellowship—in secular institutions of society.

The task of the church, as we discovered earlier, is reconciliation. Human life so easily falls back on self or group interests to the neglect of others. The church should be the inspirer of unity among men and nations. It should discover fresh ways to make that message compelling and effective.

The church thus has both an inward and an outward task. Inwardly, it must be an intense model of the true Christian community, demonstrating the life of faith, hope, and love. Outwardly, it must continuously measure secular society by these standards and seek ways to incarnate them in the concrete situations of secular life.

I suspect that if the church fails in either of these counts it will fail in both. When the life of the church is solely concentrated on itself, the church will become selfish and irrelevant, prizing only personal satisfactions for its members. When its concern is solely with the issues of the external world, the church will lose the personal meaning and dynamics that are essential to its social task. (S/R, 102.)

■ Discuss: What are the positive and negative effects on faith by organized religion? How would you answer the person who contends that one can live the life of faith outside the organized religion? What evidence do you have to support your answer?

■ Evaluate: What from this session will be most useful to you? What specific things came up that you would have liked to explore further? How could the session have been improved?

■ Close with the benediction "God Be in My Head" (Resource Packet, item 1).

■ Let the leadership team be prepared to give assignments for the next chapter of study and the members of the group be prepared to accept the assignments.

NOTES ON CHAPTER 10

Page 153: Pierre Teilhard de Chardin, *The Divine Milieu* (Harper and Row, 1960), page 35. English translation copyright © 1960 by William Collins Sons and Company, London, and Harper and Row, Publishers, Inc. Used by permission.

Page 157: Quoted in Paul L. Lehmann, *Ethics in a Christian Context* (Harper and Row, 1963), page 135. Copyright © 1963 by Paul L. Lehmann. Used by permission.

Page 158: Quoted in John Macquarrie, *Principles of Christian Theology* (Charles Scribner's Sons, 1966), page 455. Copyright © 1966 by John Macquarrie. Used by permission.

Page 158: John Macquarrie, *Principles of Christian Theology*, pages 456-57. Used by permission.

Page 162: See John C. Bennett, Howard R. Bowen, William Adams Brown, Jr., and G. Bromley Oxnam, *Christian Values and Economic Life* (Harper and Row, 1954), Chapter 4. Copyright 1954 by the Federal Council of the Churches of Christ in America.

Page 164: Philip H. Phenix, *Education and the Common Good* (Harper and Row, 1961), pages 6-7. Copyright © 1961 by Philip H. Phenix. Used by permission.

Page 164: Quoted in Philip H. Phenix, *Education and the Common Good*, page 10.

ROBERT MARKS

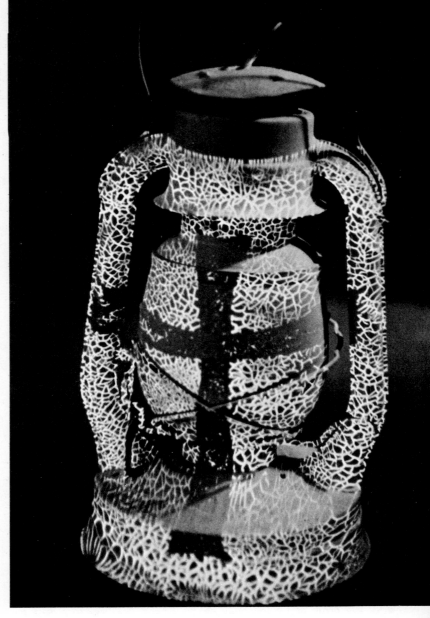

Theology is faith searching for light and understanding.

Read these selections in your Bible:

Psalms 19
God speaks to us both in nature and in our conscience.

Romans 8
The creation waits for the revealing of the sons of God.

Joshua 10:12-14
God stops the sun while Joshua slaughters his enemies.

11

□□

THEOLOGY AND THE MODERN WORLD

"The mission of the science community as I see it, is two-fold: first, to satisfy, at least in part, the fundamental human need for knowledge and understanding; and second, to improve the conditions of human existence, through the modification and partial control of physical nature and of man. This twofold task constitutes an exceedingly important part of the work of mankind. Therefore, if to be a Christian means, among other things, to accept responsibility for a full share of the world's work, it follows that . . . *one way to be a responsible Christian in the world and to express one's Chris-*

■ *As you arrive at your place of meeting, check the assignment chart for specific preparation to be made before the session begins.*

■ *Set goals for your study of this chapter as suggested on page 16.*

tian concern and to do the truth is to engage in the practice of science." *

*   *   *

In the earlier part of this book (Chapters 2-4) we traced the historical quest of the Christians seeking a definition of faith from New Testament times up through the Protestant Reformation in the sixteenth century. It is time to take up that story where we left off.

The Reformation belongs to a period of transition from medieval to modern times. In its intense religiousness, it is medieval. But in many of its themes—the emphasis upon the individual conscience and personal freedom, for instance —it is modern.

To understand our own times we must have some knowledge of the shift that took place over several centuries—the shift from the religious culture of the medieval period to the secular culture of modern times. Modern times began with the Enlightenment—the latter part of the 1700's—when "reason" came to be more highly regarded.

The change can be summarized like this. Between the medieval period and the modern period, man's center of interest shifted from heaven to earth. Man, not God, became the measure of all things. As late as the beginning of the Reformation period (early 1500's) there was a widespread concern about death and heaven. In the Enlightenment, as earlier in the Renaissance, however, interest in worldly satisfactions replaced a longing for the joys of salvation in heaven. Things in this world were real and so-called spiritual things became less and less real. The source of knowledge was no longer the Bible and the teaching of the church, but the study of the world through science.

We must understand that at least since the seventeenth century the world has become more and more secular. The major institution in the medieval world was the church. At the time of Pope Innocent III (he lived from 1160 to 1216), every prince in Christendom held his kingdom in trust from the pope. Today the major institutions are the economic, political, and technological. The church still exists and its adherents are numerous, but it does not stand in the center of our culture. Some even claim that it is saying nothing important about the events of our time. More seriously, they would claim, it has almost no influence regarding the values that individuals seek in the fulfillment of their own lives. Others believe the church *should* have nothing to say about this world except how souls can be saved. (See *S/R*, 31.)

■ Evaluate the claims of the preceding paragraph. What are specific examples of the economic, political, and technological institutions referred to? To what extent are these institutions the pace setters in today's society? What changes have come about in recent times in the relationship of the church to culture? Who is responsible for the changes: the church or culture? What factors or conditions brought about the changes? What, in your opinion, is the task of the church? to issue verbal statements in response to conditions and events of our time? to influence the value standards of individuals? to tend to the business of saving souls? What?

FOUR WAVES OF SCIENTIFIC ADVANCE

The history of the West since the time of Galileo in the seventeenth century gives the impression of continuous retreat on the part of the church. By "retreat" I mean that its influence was decreasing. With each new wave of scientific advance, the area of life left to religious control diminished.

At times, the church tried to be as graceful in retreat as the circumstances permitted. At other times, the fighting was bitter. But the advance of secularism has proceeded without slackening up to the present time. (See again *S/R*, 91.)

The major standard bearer of modern civilization has been

science. I think we will understand our modern world better if we trace briefly the four waves of scientific advance since the Reformation and note the religious reaction to them. The religious reaction was always in some sense an accommodation to the inevitable. Once scientific discoveries were made, their influence began to spread. The church opposed some of these, but inevitably it had to accept them. Theology was modified as necessary to accommodate these scientific changes. In some cases, the accommodation process resulted in the church giving up too much; as a result, the Christian message was distorted.

The first wave—astronomy and physics. Almost every school child knows the story of how Galileo (1564-1642) invented the telescope and taught that the earth revolved around the sun. To us this seems innocent enough. But to the society of Galileo's day it was a blow struck against a religious view of the world. Instead of a nice cozy earth at the center of everything, with heaven above and hell beneath, Galileo envisioned infinite space opening out into vast and immeasurable distances.

It is no wonder that the frightened churchmen of his day forced him to deny what he had been teaching. But it was all in vain; the church could not stop the spread of Galileo's discovery. Within fifty years, scarcely any educated person within Christendom would have publicly denied Galileo's vision. By this time Sir Isaac Newton (1642-1727), an English scientist, had formulated what we call classical physics with his discoveries of the laws of physical motion.

The church had to concede that in the realm of physical laws, science—not faith—was the supreme authority. (*S/R*, 103.) The earth could no longer be considered the physical center of the universe, and the discoveries of Newton suggested to some that this vast universe was governed by impersonal laws rather than a personal God.

The second wave—geology and biology. Physical science up to the time of Newton assumed that the earth and its living occupants had been created just as they presently appeared to common sense. In 1794, William Paley published a book which compared the universe to a watch. God was the "watchmaker." Paley wished to prove that the fact that the world was here presupposed a Creator. (*S/R*, 104.)

But no sooner had the accommodation of faith to science seemed assured than geologists like Sir Charles Lyell (1797-1875) began to show evidence that the earth was much older than common sense imagined and that it had been changing. Moreover, according to geology, it had been changing for millions of years.

Most theologians had put the creation of the earth at only a few thousand years before Christ. Now that date was pushed back by millions of years.

These claims of geology were harder for conservative religious minds to bear than the discoveries of Galileo and Newton. The work of geologists required a serious reexamination of the way in which the story of creation had been interpreted.

But perhaps another implication of geology was even harder to accept. I mean the notion that the earth itself was *still* changing. The idea that something remains the same is reassuring—even if it is only the ground we stand on.

After these severe shocks, an even greater one came. Biologists discovered that the species themselves, including man, are the product of a long process of change. Charles Darwin (1809-82) gave this idea its most influential formulation. (*S/R*, 105.)

The discoveries of Galileo and Newton proved that the earth was not at the center of the universe, but it was still possible to believe that God created the earth six thousand years ago (an Irish archbishop had figured the date of creation as 4004 B.C.) and that Adam was a historical person who looked very much like a man of today.

Now the new geology was teaching that the earth had come into existence millions of years ago and had slowly evolved into its present form. The new biology taught that man himself had evolved out of lower forms of life (but not from monkeys as some opponents claimed). If the earth and man had come to their present forms as a result of slow change, what happened to the biblical accounts of creation (Genesis 1–2)?

■ One person may be prepared to lead the group in an analysis of S/R, 104. As he reads the selected reading aloud, others should follow the reading carefully. Discuss this question, Can we deduce a Creator God by analogy? Using Paley's line of reasoning, point out the possible implications for belief in God as Creator.

■ Read the definition of the gospel in S/R, 106. What does the definition suggest to you about God? about creation? What does the idea of creation as unfinished or still going on suggest about God?

■ How would you express your image of creation as unfinished? Perhaps your group would like to try one of these possibilities: (1) The leadership team may provide drawing paper and water colors or colored chalk for members of the class to draw their idea of continuing creation. Finger painting would offer exciting possibilities here. (2) Plan a photo display illustrating the idea that creation is unfinished. Illustrations might include photos such as the water cycle or the seed cycle. (3) Arrange an exhibit of archaeological artifacts.

The third wave—the historical revolution. The third wave of scientific advance applied the principles of change to history and to social institutions. (S/R, 107.) Everything seemed to be changing! Nothing was permanent. History had formerly been written to inspire readers. Now historians began to study original sources, to try to see things as they really happened. History came to be viewed as a science. The new understanding of history was applied to the Bible and the church. The Bible was interpreted as a product of historical forces. The church was interpreted sociologically instead of theologically. That is, study of it was put on a level with the study of governments and economic systems as a product of social forces.

The fourth wave—psychology. With the advent of the science of psychology, science now reached into the mind of man. Human consciousness was interpreted as a product of natural forces. Perhaps the most famous name in this phase of psychological advance is Sigmund Freud (1856-1939). (*S/R*, 108.)

WHAT DID ALL THIS MEAN?

The old certainties by which men had governed their lives before the age of science seemed to be gradually swept away by this flood of new knowledge. Of course, this did not all happen at once. "The mediaeval world-view," as Alan Richardson, one of our best biblical scholars, has said, "did not disintegrate in all its parts at equal speed." *

Little by little, a new way of looking at life replaced the old way. What emerged is what I call the modern world-view or the modern mind. Some religious thinkers fought with science at each turn of the tide, but they were unable to hold it back. The history of faith during this time became more and more a time of adjusting to changes in ways of thinking brought about by science and its methods. The initiative was with the scientists, not with the theologians.

But this is perhaps to give a partially false picture. Many religious men rejoiced in the new knowledge. In fact, many of the scientists were themselves devoutly religious men and felt that they were doing God's work in uncovering new truth about his creation. Many of them also felt that the new knowledge was making even more evident some of the old truths about faith. Sir Isaac Newton himself was a religious man. The great physicist and chemist Robert Boyle (1627-91) found that the scientific contemplation of nature lifted his mind continually toward God.

Erasmus Darwin, grandfather of Charles, asked:

> Dull atheist, could a giddy dance
> Of atoms lawlessly hurl'd
> Construct so wonderful, so wise,
> So harmonised a world?

Charles Darwin himself, at least at the time of writing *Origin of Species* (1859), thought his conclusions were consistent with faith. In the final chapter he wrote:

> I see no good reason why the views given in this volume should shock the religious feelings of any one. . . . A celebrated author and divine has written to me that "he has gradually learnt to see that it is just as noble a conception of the Deity to believe that He created a few original forms capable of self-development into other and needful forms, as to believe that He required a fresh act of creation to supply the voids caused by the action of His laws."

In spite of these testimonies and others like them, the major tendency of theology was to modify traditional religious teaching in order to accommodate it to the new science. In many cases, this renewed study of Christian belief brought to light elements in faith that had been neglected. The wonder of the natural order, for instance, was revealed in a new depth by science.

But there were losses as well. Some persons found it harder to believe that there was any true knowledge apart from science. The traditional claims of revelation had been discredited in so many details that the over-all claim tended to fade. The scientific idea of discovery overtook the biblical idea of God's gift of knowledge to man.

More than that, religious ideas of conduct rooted in the medieval tradition had been challenged. Men began to guide their lives by the newer knowledge. In time, with the discovery of many different cultures with all their various standards of right and wrong, the whole idea of any absolute standard became questionable.

Another change took place when science began to pay off in terms of practical invention. We are today the heirs of the enormous productivity of that technological change. This has given men the notion that they are in control of their lives. It seemed that nothing could be denied to men who were willing to apply these new powers to their own betterment. (S/R, 109.)

■ Use the chart "Waves of Scientific Advance" (Resource Packet, item 7) to guide your study of the four waves of scientific advance and the questions posed to the Christian faith by them. The Leaders' Guide in the packet contains directions for using the chart as well as questions for discussion.

THE TURNING POINT

The turning point in this tide of human advance came shortly following the first World War, which shook confidence in continuing and inevitable progress. The automatic onward march of humanity toward a good society seemed to have been seriously interrupted. With the great depression in the 1930's and the second World War in the forties, the evidence became overwhelming. Something was wrong! (S/R, 110.)

Even secular thinkers became critical of the results. Our literature began to reflect the questions. Sin again appeared as a theme. Man did not seem quite so innocent after the mass bombings and concentration camps. Robert Penn Warren wrote:

> I have long since come to the firm and considered
> conclusion
> That love, all love, all kinds, descriptions,
> and shapes,
> Is but a mask to hide the brute face of fact,
> And that fact is the immitigable ferocity of self.*

177

Many persons began to concern themselves with the fact that human life had become dehumanized after it had been cut adrift from any sure meaning or religious standard. The loss of any standard above or beyond man began to plague those who still longed for a good society.

Even in those regions of society where men were well fed and reasonably secure, the illness of anxiety and guilt seemed to undermine human happiness. Everywhere mental illness and social delinquency were on the rise.

■ Divide the class into two groups. Let one group brainstorm (list without discussion) evidences that the modern world has lost hold on meaning and value. The second group will list evidences that the modern world is moving toward meaning and value. Both groups should record their lists on newsprint.

Then, in the total group, compare the two lists. Is there any indication that some virtues of the past are lost in the present? Why do we tend to idealize the past? In what ways does the modern age seem better?

THE CHRISTIAN FAITH RECOVERS ITS VOICE

These doubts corresponded to a new investigation of the grounds of our faith. Karl Barth (pronounced *BART*) in Switzerland, for instance, and Reinhold Niebuhr (pronounced *NEE-bur*) in America rose to speak prophetically on behalf of this renewal. (Later in this chapter we shall return to a discussion of Karl Barth.)

The keynote of change was sounded in America by the great liberal preacher Harry Emerson Fosdick. Toward the end of his career in a now-celebrated sermon, delivered in 1935, he said:

The Church must go beyond modernism. We have been all things to all men long enough. We have adapted and adjusted and accommodated and conceded long enough. We have at times gotten so low down that we talked as though the highest compliment that could be paid to Almighty God was that a few scientists believed in him.*

178

Fosdick did not, nor should we, repudiate the achievements of the liberal period. "If we are successfully to maintain the thesis that the church must go beyond modernism [Fosdick said in the same sermon], we must start by seeing that the church had to go as far as modernism." *

He believed that the battle of modernizing had been largely won and felt the new watchword will not be "Accommodate yourself to the prevailing culture! but, Stand out from it and challenge it!" *

Daniel Day Williams writes about this new tone of prophetic challenge in theology.

> In the modern period of Christianity there was an emphasis on the question, "How can the Christian faith be made intelligible within and in harmony with the highest idealism and scientific thought of our civilization?" Now the question is, "What is there in the Christian faith which gives us such an understanding of ourselves that we must assert our loyalty to the Holy God above all the splendid and yet corruptible values of our civilization?" *

On this new understanding of the faith, what happens to our view of science? Does this new recovery of faith cancel out three hundred years of scientific advance? Far from it! It restores faith and science to a true partnership. During the period in which faith tried so hard to accommodate to science, many of the profound truths of our faith were neglected or forgotten. Now that modern man is discovering that in spite of scientific progress he cannot get on very well without some meaning to his life, some standard for his value judgments, and some ground for his personal and social existence, he is ready to hear the word of faith again.

And that word is itself purified by having been shorn of medieval and other cultural accumulations that did not belong to the Christian faith in the first place. The search for a prophetic word has sent us back to Christian origins in the great period of the Reformation and back beyond that to the New Testament itself.

179

We are now prepared to see the true nature of the scientific achievement. Science is no longer to be viewed as the sole source of truth or the power by which men may save themselves. Science is the means of understanding a significant aspect of human life, but it is the servant, not the lord.

We now understand that scientific knowledge does not compete with faith. (*S/R*, 111.) Scientific knowledge helps us describe the physical world and its laws. But it gives us no understanding of the world's ultimate meaning. We can describe social systems, but we cannot derive solely from that description an ethic to guide our lives. Understanding of ultimate meaning and guidance for life emerge out of trustful participation in doing the will of God.

As a result of this newer perspective, for instance, the old quarrels that raged over the creation accounts in the Book of Genesis are now seen in a new light. These accounts were not written to compete with science. Their message expresses the meaning of creation and the wonder that God brought it about in the first place. The Genesis accounts tell us that this world is a place of utmost importance and that life is a trust from the Most High. Questions about the order in which living things appeared, or the amount of time they took, and so on, are not a central concern to faith.

We know now that the Bible is not a textbook of physical facts. It contains views about the physical world common to the beliefs of the ancient peoples among whom the biblical books were written. We also know that the prescientific views in no way affect the Bible as a word of authority for faith. The important teaching for faith of Joshua 10:12-14, for example, is not that the sun stood still but that the people knew God was with them in a time of crisis.

■ Listen as one person reads aloud Joshua 10:6-14. What is the central message of this passage? Can one believe that God was with the Israelites in this situation and *not* believe the sun stood still? Explain. What principles of interpretation are involved?

No longer need men of faith worry about whether some new scientific theory is going to contradict some teaching of faith. Science often gives us tools to help faith become active in the world. As the scientist James Bryant Conant says, science can give the Good Samaritan a helping hand. With medicine, for instance, think of how good men can help others in ways not possible in former ages. We can give thanks to God daily for science and promote it with our whole hearts. And we can give thanks to God for our faith and the guidance it gives to our lives. Those concerned with "doing theology" can appreciate the value of science. (S/R, 112.)

CURRENT MOVEMENTS IN THEOLOGY

Theology is still alive with all sorts of vigorous debate over important issues. You might think that after all these centuries something should have been settled.

Sometimes people have a very doubtful notion: they believe that the theology of the past is good enough for them. (S/R, 113.) "What was good enough for my grandfather is good enough for me." Sometimes they say, "What was good enough for Paul is good enough for me." This assumes two doubtful things. The first is that they know what Paul (or their grandfather) really thought. The second is that Paul (or grandfather) had thought through all the implications of the Christian faith for every age.

If they mean that the *faith* of Paul is good enough for them, I would agree. I would say that it is more than good enough— it probably far exceeds our faith. But as we have seen, theology is not faith. Theology is an attempt to make clear to ourselves what our faith means.

According to this view, every age must develop a theology of its own; that is, it must restate the meaning of the Christian faith for its own day. Augustine, Luther, and Wesley

181

developed their theology in light of their situation. We must try to do for our age what they did for theirs.

Faith must never stop searching for understanding. Every age has to rethink its theology in the setting in which it lives. To fail to relate faith and the events of the world in which we live would be to fail in our duty toward Christ.

So in this final chapter we are going to notice very briefly some of the current movements in theology. We cannot notice them all, and we cannot go very deeply into any one of them. But this quick survey should at least alert us to lines of thought that will be worth following up on our own.

■ Form groups of three or four persons to discuss this question: When people speak of the "old-time religion," what do they have in mind? Each group should record its responses on newsprint. Now contrast this with "new-time religion" or current theological thinking. What differences are there? Is wishing for the old like the wish to be a child again? In what ways? How might idealizing religion of the past be a means of avoiding confrontation of the Christian faith with the issues and concerns of today's world? Why is the "old-time religion" less threatening to some people than "new-time religion"? What is the significance of the fact that the good days are always in the past, never the present? See *S/R,* 113.

THE RECOVERY OF BIBLICAL FAITH

Modern theologians are very interested in the Bible. Perhaps Karl Barth (mentioned earlier in this chapter) has done as much as any single theologian in our time to call attention to the importance of the Bible. Barth saw in the days after World War I that what was needed was greater attention to the biblical message. In the periods of disillusionment through the 1920's, 30's, and 40's, enormous energy was devoted to the attempt to rediscover the message of the Bible for our time. One American biblical scholar expressed the renewed interest in the 1950's in this way:

The Bible is meant to be read and understood in times like these. The literature of the Old and New Testaments is the deposit

182

of a succession of historical crises in which men were faced with the question of the meaning of their existence. With stark realism the Bible describes events which rocked the very foundation of life, which destroyed nations and displaced populations, which wrought havoc, suffering, and anxiety. This drama of faith was enacted upon a stage where poor people were the victims of the rich, where Palestinian rulers were drawn into the maelstrom of international events, and where one great nation after another sought to create a world empire by the power of the sword. Situated strategically at the crossroads of the ancient world, Palestine was the very storm center of life. The Bible, therefore, does not come from a sheltered valley of Shangri-la; its message was forged out of circumstances in which people felt the maximum of tension and suffering. This book speaks out of the immediate and concrete realities of history, where men doubted and believed, hated and loved, despaired and hoped. Its message comes from the depth of life and speaks to the depth within us. It finds us where we are living. Therefore it is understandable that as modern people wrestle with the issues of destiny in their own contemporary situation, they often find themselves in rapport with the prophets and apostles of the Bible. Perhaps the Bible is most deeply understood only by shipwrecked men.*

DE-MYTHOLOGIZING

Do not be put off by the strange word. Its meaning is quite simple. Rudolf Bultmann discovered in his study of the New Testament that the message of the Bible is embedded in the picture of the world of the people living at the times when the biblical books were written. These world-pictures he calls myths. His point is that the permanent Bible message must be lifted out of this ancient world-picture so that modern men *do not confuse the world-picture with the message itself.* Notice that Bultmann is not saying that the Bible is a myth; he says that the world-picture is mythical. (S/R, 114.)

Here is an example of what Bultmann means by mythical language in the Bible. The Bible speaks of Jesus coming "down" from heaven for earthly mission and then going back "up" after the Resurrection. This carries with it a picture of heaven as a place in the sky. The Apostles' Creed also contains a phrase about "descending" into hell. (This phrase is omitted in the "Methodist version" of the creed.) This statement suggests another place under our feet where men are punished for their sins.

Bultmann does not deny that heaven and hell stand for real truths in our faith. What he denies is that we must accept the three-story universe of heaven "up there," earth "here," and hell "down there."

Bultmann wants to help us see that, in order to understand the message of the Bible, we must distinguish between the core of meaning of that message and the first-century thought forms in which it is expressed. Persons living in the time of Jesus believed the earth was flat. The universe had three stories or levels. The earth was the middle or lower story; hell was like a cellar or basement below it; and heaven was the upper story. Bultmann wants to help us see the *meaning* of the New Testament teaching about, for instance, hell, even though we may not believe hell is literally a place below the surface of the ground. This is what he means when he says we cannot fully understand what the New Testament is about until we "de-mythologize" it. We must try, as far as possible, to put ourselves in the place of the first-century person when we read.

How does this process work out, this "de-mythologizing"? To continue the discussion of hell as an example, Bultmann urges us to try to understand the minds of the first-century audience. These people who listened to Jesus and to the preachers of the early church literally did believe that the fire was under their feet. But that is not the point of what Jesus was teaching; he wanted to convey that the worst thing about hell was that it was the most painful imaginable separation from God. Stated in terms like this, the reader in the twentieth century can readily understand the point, even though he may not believe hell is underground.

■ Take time to understand the term *de-mythologizing*. Let one or two persons state aloud their understanding of Bultmann's use of the terms *myth* and *world-picture*. One person may be ready to distinguish between Bultmann's meaning for *myth* and the dictionary definition of the word.

Modern-day students of Scripture must constantly put themselves in the place of the first-century Christian. To gain some understanding of the necessity of this process, imagine that you are living a thousand years from today. What kinds of information would you need in order to understand the historical accounts of the twentieth century? List these on newsprint.

Working in groups of four or five persons, practice the concept of de-mythologizing. Study one of these passages: Mark 5:1-20; Matthew 4:1-11. Ask these questions: What is the core of the message? What part of the passage is the world-picture in which the message is set? You may wish to refer to the chart "Study a Portion of the Bible" (Resource Packet, *God With Us,* item 2).

EXISTENTIALISM

Existentialism is a way of thinking that puts man and his problems first and theoretical questions second. Specifically, this view means that existentialists concentrate on such questions as man's freedom and responsibility, his guilt and anxieties, and his search for a meaning to life.

Paul Tillich once said that existentialism was the "good luck of modern theology." He meant that this way of thinking helped theology in its work of understanding faith.

The meaning of existentialism is clearer when we see the use that Bultmann makes of it in talking about the message of the Bible. He says that the concern of the New Testament is not to confront man with a theory of the universe but with a choice between two radically different ways of existing as a human being. The first way is outside of faith. Outside of faith, an individual must contrive ways and means out of his own resources of saving himself. He must create on his own, for instance, the meaning of his life, the standards by which he will decide important questions, and so on.

The second way is the way of faith. This way calls man

to give up all self-contrived efforts at solving the problems of existence—his guilt and anxiety, for instance—and to trust God with his life. This way means letting go of all visible realities and opening one's self to the forgiving grace of God. Thus a man finds release from his own past and from all fear of the future. This kind of trusting life Bultmann calls true existence. (S/R, 115 and 116.)

The Bible, says Bultmann, warns us that the first way of existing is bound to fail. Man cannot save himself. He cannot manage guilt and anxiety. He cannot create his own meaning. He cannot find within himself a center for freedom. The offer of God in Christ is the solution to these problems of existence.

It is not necessary to believe the specific biblical view of the physical world in order to accept this message of hope. The message and the forms in which it is expressed are not logically tied together.

It is, thus, that de-mythologizing coupled with existentialism tries to release in our day the biblical message and lets it do its saving work again.

■ Use again Bulletin Board Display IV (Resource Packet, item 2). In the light of the preceding discussion, what choice of ways of existing is offered these persons? What does this interpretation of existentialism offer these persons? What response is necessary for these persons to experience "true existence"?

THE THEOLOGY OF LANGUAGE

We have seen how Bultmann and others have learned from the current philosophy known as existentialism. Another movement of great influence on theology is interested in the analysis of the language we use. Perhaps an illustration will help.

Consider two sentences: "Jesus was the Son of God." "John the Baptist was the son of Zechariah." Grammatically, these

two sentences are the same. But it would be a mistake to think
that the logic of the two sentences is the same. "Son of" does
not mean the same thing in these two sentences. How could
it? Was God a "father" in the exact same sense in which a
human being is a father? Are we to think of God begetting a
son in the same way that Zechariah begat John?

No doubt, in both cases we want to say that the son bears
his father's characteristics. But even here the meaning is
surely different. If fact, we often say when a fine man has
an evil son that the boy is not a "true son of his father."

Many theological misunderstandings could be removed or.
diminished if we realized that we are forced to use *ordinary*
language in an *unusual* way when we talk about God, Christ,
the Holy Spirit, or other facts of our spiritual existence. How
many futile arguments have arisen over trying to prove that
Jesus is the "son of God." Proof in theological matters is
very different from proof in ordinary affairs. We know the
kind of biological testing by which today we can prove that
A is the son of B. But what kind of evidence is appropriate
to proving that Jesus is the son of God? Wherever such
"proofs" appear, they simply express the *faith* of the speaker.
(*S/R,* 117.)

Theologians tell us that it is much better to realize that
such "proofs" do not really draw people to God. We should
speak rather of "witnessing" to our faith rather than trying
to "prove" it with arguments. Witnessing does indeed per-
suade skeptics, turns them into believers, even when argument fails.

Of course, as we have seen, intelligence must witness to
the faith as well. And this means spelling out the faith in
coherent (reasonable) terms, as far as we are able. But this
is not the same as objective proof. Objective proof only works
with objects, not with the content of faith. We could say
why we believe someone is our friend, but we would not

regard this belief as "proof." Friendship verifies itself in life experiences with the friend.

THE "DEATH" OF GOD

The expression "God is dead" has become well known in our time. It is shocking enough to provoke a considerable stir and some violent reaction. This slogan points to another element in the theology of our day. Let me call it, for convenience, "worldly holiness." It will be necessary to sort out the various strands in this complex theme.

The major development of modern times that has led thinkers to take the "God is dead" theme seriously is the steady movement of Western society toward secularism. What does this mean? (*S/R*, 118.)

Its meaning can best be seen by contrasting the religious character of medieval culture with our own culture. In the Middle Ages everything was related to faith. The paintings were of themes of faith. The greatest buildings were cathedrals. The themes of the literature were mostly biblical. Theology was regarded as the queen of the sciences. Everything in that culture testified to an interest in God, Christ, heaven, and hell. Even political and economic activity were under religious law.

By contrast, the themes of our art and literature are of this world, dealing with man rather than God. Our greatest buildings are dedicated to worldly purposes. Our governments and economies, separated from the jurisdiction of the church, are justified by secular theories. Our ethics are completely separate from thoughts of heaven and hell and concentrate upon making life better here and now.

We can perhaps see this secularizing trend best by asking what institutions affect our lives most. Are they not business and government? In a list of organizations most seriously influencing the course of the major events of our time the church would certainly be far down the list.

The expression "God is dead" may simply mean this diminishing effect of religious influences in our time.

Two alternative interpretations are possible. One interpretation says that we have learned to do well enough without faith. Science, government, and education can save us. All the problems we face must be dealt with in political, economic, or educational terms. Ethics and morals must be interpreted in strictly human terms. Man is the measure of all things.

The second interpretation seems to mean that the Christian should accept the secular work as God's providence. That is, God has allowed us to grow up into a kind of maturity and independence that does not need to lean on him as a crutch. The true place of faith will emerge only after we have learned to accept our maturity and reject all false kinds of immature religiousness. (S/R, 119.)

Another way of putting this second view would be to say, in terms that I have used in the earlier part of this book, that God intends to incarnate himself in our total life. The presence of God in the man Jesus is the model. This means that we must find in every case what God means in terms of economics, education, political affairs, and so on. This would be true "secular meaning of the Gospel." *

The first interpretation mentioned earlier in this section leads to a humanism that rejects the whole idea of God or any faith in a power for good beyond man. The second interpretation leads to a fulfillment of the meaning of the Christian faith if we interpret it incarnationally. In this second way of thinking, God's purpose in Christ is not to produce a *religious* person but a *true human being*. It would insist that a true human being is impossible without faith in God.

There are many dimensions to this second interpretation.

We can only suggest a few of them here. One is that the Christian should not be church-centered. The church has its function, but only as a *means* to a complete humanity under God. God's sovereignty is not over the church alone but over all of man's life. God does not care more for the church than for businesses, governments, hospitals, schools, and the like. God's concern is for the whole of human life, not just the "religious" part. If we look closely at the Old Testament, we discover that this is the way the prophets looked at their world. They were concerned primarily with social justice, foreign policy, and human relationships. They spoke about temple worship and such things, but only as a means of clarifying this larger concern. Idolatry was denounced as the means by which men deluded themselves with a false religiousness so that they could go on cheating, robbing, and ignoring the needs of their fellow human beings.

This prophetic way of thinking is the background for the New Testament ethic of love. It underscores Jesus' own refusal to put sacred practices, such as sabbath observance, above human needs. After all, we must recall that he was put to death for his "antireligiousness," according to the religious people of his time. The indictment was blasphemy.

This line of thought helps us put private devotion and religious worship into their proper places. If worship is an excuse for withdrawal into a separate sphere, it opposes God's purposes for our life. Worship and devotion, properly understood, can deepen our understanding of God's total sovereignty over all of our life. It can send us out as men among men to live the secular life with a vertical dimension that enables us to continually transform it into the dimensions of God's kingdom. Our full Christian task is the transformation of the earth, not the building of churches. (*S/R*, 120).

■ Let a panel of four persons be prepared to discuss issues related to the "God is dead" expression. They may deal with these questions in relation to the above discussion and interpretation: What is meant here by secularism? What factors contributed to the difference in attitude toward religion in the Middle Ages and in the twentieth century? What fallacies or truths appear in any one of the interpretations? What is meant by God's intent to incarnate himself in our total life? How would you describe a "true human being"? In light of the above discussion about the church, what, in your opinion, is the place of the church in the life of a Christian? Panel members should consult the selected readings in this section for additional ideas. Allow time for group reaction.

■ As a means of reviewing ideas that have been discussed in Chapters 6-11, use side two of the chart "What Have You Learned?" (Resource Packet, item 6). The Leaders' Guide in the packet includes specific directions for using the chart.

■ Evaluate your study of this unit in light of the Objective of Christian Education, S/R, 100. Ask these questions about each section of the objective: How has our study of theology helped us move toward this goal? Where have we been hindered in making progress toward this goal?

■ Persons who have been keeping a theological diary throughout this study may wish to share what they have learned about themselves and their faith through this activity. Also you may wish to repeat the first procedure suggested on page 26 of Chapter 1.

■ Use as your benediction "God Be in My Head" (Resource Packet, item 1).

■ The author and the editors hope you have used the materials and suggestions of this unit freely. We hope you have taken more than a quarter for your study. If you do have time for another session before beginning the fifth unit of Foundation Studies, we suggest you go back and try some of the procedures you omitted. Or read together some of the selected readings you missed, or repeat some procedures that might have more meaning for you now.

NOTES ON CHAPTER 11

Page 169-70: Harold K. Schilling, *Science With Christian Concern* (The Board of Education of The Methodist Church, 1964), page 3. Copyright 1964 by The Board of Education of The Methodist Church. Used by permission.

Page 175: Alan Richardson, *The Bible in the Age of Science* (Westminster Press, 1961), page 41. Copyright © 1961 by S.C.M. Press. Used by permission.

191

Page 177: Robert Penn Warren, *Brother to Dragons* (Random House, 1953), page 41. Copyright 1953 by Robert Penn Warren. Used by permission.

Page 178: Harry Emerson Fosdick, "Beyond Modernism," *The Christian Century,* December 4, 1935, page 1552. Copyright by the Christian Century Foundation. Used by permission.

Page 179: *The Christian Century,* December 4, 1935, page 1549. Used by permission.

Page 179: *The Christian Century,* December 4, 1935, page 1552. Used by permission.

Page 179: Daniel Day Williams, *What Present-Day Theologians Are Thinking* (Harper and Row, 1959, revised edition), page 18. Copyright © 1952, 1959 by Daniel Day Williams. Used by permission.

Pages 182-83: Bernhard W. Anderson, *Rediscovering the Bible* (Association Press, 1951), pages 5-6. Copyright 1951 by Haddam House. Used by permission.

Page 189: See Paul M. Van Buren, *Secular Meaning of the Gospel* (Macmillan Company, 1963).